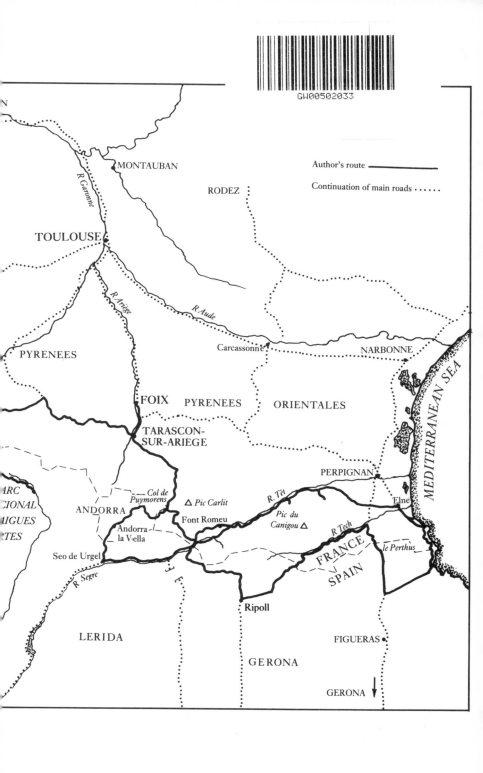

GW00502033

MONTAUBAN

RODEZ

Author's route ————
Continuation of main roads ······

R Garonne

TOULOUSE

R Ariège

R Aude

PYRENEES

Carcassonne

NARBONNE

MEDITERRANEAN SEA

FOIX    PYRENEES    ORIENTALES

TARASCON-
SUR-ARIEGE

PERPIGNAN

PARC
CIONAL
IGUES
TES

Col de
Puymorens    △ Pic Carlit    R. Têt    Elne

ANDORRA    Font Romeu    Pic du
Canigou △

Andorra-
la Vella    R Tech

FRANCE    le Perthus

Seo de Urgel    SPAIN

R. Segre

LERIDA    Ripoll    FIGUERAS

GERONA

GERONA ↓

# THE PYRENEES

# THE PYRENEES

*Roger Higham*

COLUMBUS BOOKS
LONDON

First published in Great Britain in 1988 by
Columbus Books Limited
19-23 Ludgate Hill,
London EC4M 7PD


Copyright © 1988 Roger Higham
Line drawings copyright © 1988 Roger Higham
Chapter decoration by Vera Brice
Photographs are reproduced courtesy of the French Government Tourist Office
and the Spanish National Tourist Office

British Library Cataloguing in Publication Data

Higham, Roger
    The Pyrenees.—— (Travelscapes).
    1. Europe. Pyrenees. —— Description and travel
    —— Visitors' guides
    I. Title
    914.6′520483

ISBN 0-86287-323-1

Designed by Vera Brice
Maps by Vera Brice and Leslie Robinson
Set in Linotron Ehrhardt by Facet Film Composing Limited
Leigh-on-Sea, Essex
Printed and bound by Richard Clay Ltd, Bungay, Suffolk

*To Fiona*

# CONTENTS

# ILLUSTRATIONS

## PLATES

## LINE DRAWINGS

# MAPS

The following symbols are used
in the maps:
   ✝   Church or monastery
   ♜   Castle
   ∴   Ancient monument
   △   Mountain peak
   ⊻   Viewpoint
   Υ   Waterfall
   ✳   Lighthouse

# Preface

Most people, and even some school-children, know that the Pyrenees are mountains which separate France from Spain. They dimly realize also that these mountains are not giants like some of the Alps and most of the Himalayas, and that their potential for winter-sporting is often dismissed by enthusiasts as second-rate. Yet the winter is not the best time to see the Pyrenees and if a traveller were to visit the range in warmer seasons he would see some of the most dramatic scenery in Europe. At any time of year, though, he would find a diversity of inhabitants including two highly individual races who are neither Spanish nor French, and an historical background so full of incident that scarcely a village straggles up a mountainside that has no haunting memories.

There are also diverse ways of paying one's visit: there are Pyrenean fringe towns, such as Bayonne, Pamplona, Lourdes, Pau, Bagnères de Luchon, in which one could stay and tour daily; there are smaller towns, yet with comfortable hotels, from one end to the other, for a progressive tour: there are camping-sites for the caravanner; there are hundreds of miles of completely uninhabited countryside, unimaginably beautiful, for the keen and intrepid walker; there are uncomputable combinations of all of these.

If it be objected that the Pyrenees consist merely of a huge wall between one country and another and as such have no particular fascination, as have, say, the complexities of the Swiss Alps, then it must be said that this is a misconception.

The Pyrenees are not a single range, they are a mountain system whose watershed does not extend from one side, the west, to the other, the east. There are two lines which form the axis, neither of which runs due west to east and there is a gap in the middle, like that of a sparkplug, where they do not meet. In that gap, aptly enough, there is an anomaly: a piece of Spain which geographically ought to be in France.

On the northern side of this broken axis there are deep indentations caused by torrential rivers which rose in the watershed, cut chasms in the rock and rushed down to the plains of France and emptied themselves, mainly in the Atlantic Ocean, partly in the Mediterranean Sea. From France, therefore, the Pyrenees appear as a sharply serrated, formidable and spectacular outline, a silhouette of breath-taking majesty. South of the watershed the picture is vastly more confused, a chaotic jumble of subsidiary ranges which run, on the whole, parallel to the axis. Rivers on this side, like the Arga, the Aragon, the Segre, descend as far as they can and then, diverted by the lateral ranges, run east or west for miles before they can find their way to the great plain of the Ebro, or the Mediterranean. Accordingly there is no view of the Pyrenees in Spain half so dramatic as that seen almost anywhere from the French side.

But the sheer complexity of valleys on the Spanish side has contributed to the unique quality of their habitation: so high are the hills, so difficult of access every valley, that each tends to have its own personality, its own dialect and customs.

In the centre, the mountains are impassable: there is still no route for motor traffic between Pourtalet, north-east of Jaca in the west, and Puymorens, at the head of the Ariège valley in the east. This factor is the reason for the distribution of the population.

The Basques straddle the western end of the range, where there are easy passes – Maya, Roncesvalles, Somport and the more difficult Pourtalet – which have enabled communities to remain in contact with each other and to maintain both their stolid resistance to interference by the two countries which govern them and their insistence on 'Euskadi Bat': the Basques united.

East of the last Basque valleys, with no passes over the watershed, the counties of Béarn and Foix developed on the French side, and the strong kingdom of Aragon on the Spanish. Where the axis becomes again passable, so at once another race, the Catalans, straddle it. The county of Roussillon in France and that of the great mountain-ringed valley of the Cerdanya, in both France and Spain, comprise a part of Catalonia; and Catalans, like the Basques, are jealous of their individuality. Over the Eastern Pyrenees, divided politically into areas under French or Spanish control, flies the red-and-yellow flag of the Catalans, oblivious of this technical partition. Then there is the tiny enclosed valley of Andorra, owing sovereignty in theory to both Spain and France but, in fact, autonomous.

Historically, the Pyrenean peoples played a vital part in the long struggle to keep the Muslim Moors first at bay, then at a greater distance, and finally out of Spain altogether. The Spanish Marches, the border between Christian France and Mohamme-dan Spain, lay approximately along the whole mountain range. The long struggle between Christian and Muslim (known as 'the Paynim' in the Middle Ages) elicited a great mass of romantic literature, like the 'Song of Roland'. Yet the majority of it was produced by writers unconnected personally with the region. The Pyrenean people themselves tended to accept their Muslim neighbours and to communicate with them, substituting pragmatic commerce for idealistic hostility. No wonder, therefore, that the 'struggle' did take such a very long time.

Christianity prevailed, and its influence, demonstrated by countless churches and monasteries built in the securer days of the eleventh and twelfth centuries in the style known as romanesque, pervades the entire range and provides a solid cultural background to its peoples, so diverse in other ways. It might be this cultural background, or the ethnic origins of the people, or the scenic beauty, or a combination of all these ingredients which inspired the musicians, poets, authors and painters of the Pyrenees. Many are celebrated and will be encountered in their turn; very many more are not, being local and anonymous, but have left their songs and dances to be performed at the Pyrenean festivals every year, affairs of colour, vivacity and huge enjoyment for the participants, whether local or tourist.

The route taken in this book progresses from west to east, Atlantic to Mediterannean, then back to Andorra. The reasons for this are simple. The mountains are lower in the west, higher towards the east, so a journey in that direction gives a sense of rising climax as the heights increase in grandeur. Geography explains the choice of route: using the deep valleys and western passes, there is a zig-zag progress, north to south to north, until there are no more passes, whereon the zig-zag continues on the northern, French side. There is a lateral plunge to visit Val d'Aran, then the zig-zag again until the Ariège can be followed to the pass of Puymorens at its head. From this point eastwards there are two valleys, both tracing a course eastward to the Mediterranean, and both essential viewing. Our route, therefore, follows the northern river, the Têt, down to the coast, and the southern, the Tech, back up into the mountains to the Cerdanya plain. The Grande Finale is provided by penetration of the exotic curiosity of Andorra, and the exciting climb out of it by the highest pass in the whole system, back into France.

I should like to mention here, in case readers fear that their cars' engine capacities might not rise to the rigours of Pyrenean motoring, that ours was a two-year-old Ford Fiesta Popular, with a 950 c.c. engine. It coped happily with the worst of the roads and the most difficult of the passes, and never gave us a minute's trouble.

# 1

# *The Landes to the Porte de Maya*

The strip of coastal country between Bordeaux and Bayonne is known as the Landes. The word means heath, or moorland, and that is what it used to be. But King Louis XVI in the eighteenth century caused it to be planted with coniferous trees, changing its character totally. It is a strange place, with its own atmosphere, some delightful villages, people who are born hunters and are normally to be seen with boots on their feet, bandolier across one shoulder and gun in hand, and roads which run straight as a die for miles at a stretch. I walked through it once, camping, and it took me a week. The smells of the trees, their leaves, of woodsmoke, of pine-needles; and the sounds, of the ubiquitous *tronconneuses*, the chain-saws that gave the Landais their chief source of income, of the early-morning cock-crow and the endless barking of farm dogs – these return to me still.

My wife Fiona and I drove through these long straight roads, one morning late in March, in pouring rain. Mid-winter apart, March and April are probably the worst season of the year for travelling in the Pyrenees, and this year, the winter having been not only severe but also protracted beyond its usual length, was worse than most. But for various reasons we had no alternative, so were obliged to make the best of it.

The pine forests bordering the Nationale 10 at last gave way to the outskirts of St-Esprit, northern suburb of Bayonne. We crossed the bridge over the swirling Adour and parked by the river-side. The rain had stopped, the morning was cloudy and cool, the city streets not thronged because it was Sunday. Shops were shut, except for grocers, butchers and confectioners, the latter displaying miraculous designs in Bayonne chocolate, ready for Easter. We wandered through the deeply arcaded, narrow streets, to Rue Thiers, where the Château-Vieux stands on one side, and a little farther up on the left, the fine Gothic cathedral of Ste-Marie.

Bayonne is reckoned to be a Basque capital and it has a Basque name, Baï-ona, which means Good River; but it serves equally the Landais from farther north and the Béarnais from farther east. The town stands on the River Adour, a few miles from the ea, and from earliest times its prosperity has depended on the navigability of the river-mouth. 'Gaul comprises three areas,' says Caesar in his Gallic Wars, 'inhabited respectively by the Belgae, the Aquitani, and a people who call themselves Celts, though we call them Gauls.'

From the early days of the Roman Empire, after Caesar's conquest of Gaul and the assumption of imperial power by his nephew Octavian, later known as Augustus, there comes a picture of the Novem populi, the Nine Peoples, of the Aquitani who inhabited the area between the Garonne, which empties into the sea at Bordeaux, and the Pyrenees. Some of these tribal groups held the plains of the Garonne farther north. One of them, the Tarbelli, occupied the Landes and the lower Adour and Garonne valleys: they were the builders of Bayonne, which was known to the Romans as Lapurdum.

The Romans give us no information on the Basques, who occupied then precisely the area they occupy today, but it is they who give the modern city its character. In 1120 they procured from the Duke of Aquitaine a charter of self-government. In 1154 the Duke of Aquitaine (young Henry Plantagenet of Anjou, who married the heiress of the last duke) became King of

England as Henry II, so Bayonne began a long and profitable commercial link with England.

The Plantagenet link is still evident, both in a plaque on the wall of the Château-Vieux, and in the cathedral. Built on the rising ground at the point where the Nive comes to join the Adour, the **Château-Vieux** was sited on a naturally defensible spot. The present walls may be comparatively modern, but the site was used first by the Tarbelli, then the Romans when Lapurdum was a fortress and trading port, and then by successive dukes, viscounts and kings:

> Don Alonso the Warrior, King of Navarre (1130); the Black Prince; du Guesclin and Don Pedro the Cruel, King of Castille (1367); King Louis XI (1463); King François I (1526); King Charles IX (1565); King Louis XIV (1660); Marie-Anne de Neuborg, Queen of Spain (1706); and General Palafox (1809).

These are all leading players in the long-running drama of the history of France. The Plantagenet Edward, Prince of Wales, governed Gascony for his father King Edward III in the 1350s and 1360s, and earned a reputation which caused him to be called *le prince noir*, a name normally reserved for the Devil. The castle was re-shaped in the late seventeenth century by the great military engineer, Vauban, and although I have seen it (in the 1960s) used as a barracks for 'les Paras', it is now full of residential apartments.

The **Cathedral of Ste-Marie** was begun in the thirteenth century, and that period's characteristic pointed arches separate the nave from the aisles. Due to Revolutionary vandalism, however, much of the fabric has had to be restored, including the addition of the twin spires in the nineteenth century. One thirteenth-century survivor is the door-knocker on the north door known as the 'ring of sanctuary', because in that age a fugitive from the law could claim sanctuary as soon as his hand touched it. There is also a beautifully carved doorway on the south arm of the transept. Another survivor of the Revolution is a

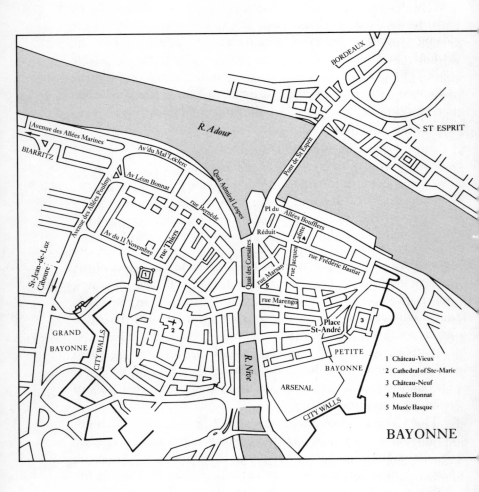

BAYONNE

1 Château-Vieux
2 Cathedral of Ste-Marie
3 Château-Neuf
4 Musée Bonnat
5 Musée Basque

stained-glass window dated 1531, in the same Renaissance style as others which have been restored. The Plantagenet link is provided by one of the bosses in the centre of each joint of the vaulted ceiling: shields bearing coats of arms decorate them, and by peering dimly up to the heights you can just make out the three crouching leopards on red which still form a part of the royal arms of the United Kingdom.

We walked round the great apse, our footsteps the only sound until the howling of a baby being baptized in one of the side chapels broke the spell. A mass was to be celebrated at 11.30, so we left the darkness of the nave for the pale sunlight in the cloisters. They have been much restored, but their colonnades preserve their fourteenth-century tracery and vaulting, and from their far side we could see the graceful flying buttresses that support the cathedral's walls, and its twin spires.

Across the swirling Nive and on the far side of Place St-André is the weed-grown, semi-derelict Château-Neuf. Sad and shabby now, it has been in turn the headquarters of the 49th Infantry Regiment and the 8th Para Division. At one time, but no longer, the streets of Bayonne were full of the famous Paras, with their red berets and shoulders full of coloured cords. Bayonne has a strong military tradition. In addition to the Châteaux Vieux and Neuf, there is a mighty citadel on the north bank, behind the quarter of St-Esprit, whose walls can be seen high on the cliff-top overlooking the river: it was built by the great Vauban in the 1680s and besieged by the Duke of Wellington's troops when they invaded France in 1814. Already by then Bayonne was flourishing as a free port, with a re-opened sea-channel, a fishing fleet bringing back rich harvests of whales from Newfoundland, and a steady export of iron goods. One of the items included in the latter was a type of short sword which could be fitted on the end of a musket-barrel: the word bayonette is known internationally, and personally to every infantryman. A poet, Tristan Derème, sighing after some lost love like all good poets, found a useful metaphor:

L'oeil de la Bayonnaise est une baionette,
Adour, cruel Adour, quand tu nous tiens!

Bayonne is also famous, rather more agreeably, not only for its chocolate but also for its ham, which appears in variable proportions in 'les sandwichs' of the locality.

The art gallery of Bayonne is **Musée Bonnat**, housed in a fine classical building, built in 1896, in rue Frédéric Bastiat. Léon Bonnat was born in Bayonne (in 1833; he died in 1922), was a painter and taught in the Ecole des Beaux-Arts in Paris. Among his pupils were the Post-Impressionists Toulouse-Lautrec, Munch, Braque and Dufy. His own work was in portraiture. Some of his large, full-length works hang in the elegant ground floor, such as his 'Portrait of a Lady' in a shimmering silvery ball-gown. When Bonnat gave his entire collection to the town of Bayonne, the council responded by building the gallery to accommodate it. When we visited it, redecoration was in progress and enough had been completed to see that the pictures will have a still more stylish setting. As the first floor was then all ladders, drapes and paint-pots, the rest of the collection was huddled into the second. One room was devoted to Rubens' sketches for paintings of biblical or classical mythological subjects. There were some Belgian tapestries and a wide diversity of other eighteenth- and nineteenth-century painters, including Poussin, El Greco, Murillo, Lawrence, Raeburn, Etty, the sketch for the Colonel Tarleton portrait by Reynolds, a Constable of Hampstead Heath, a Goya self-portrait, and some Ingres, including a portrait of the pompous King Charles X, last of the Bourbons. A semi-basement area housed Bonnat's collection of Egyptian, Greek and Roman artefacts.

Deep, cool arcades run along many of the streets of Bayonne. The ground floors are built of massive stone, the material of the columns, and the houses are of the Basque style: the upper storeys are timber-framed, with painted wooden shutters, often in bright colours, with a deep-eaved, shallow-sloping roof. Balconies and window-boxes resplendent with flowers complete the fresh, neat impression of the Basques' pride in their homes. One of these big, solid houses, near the bridge over the Nive a few hundred metres before its junction with the Adour, is the **Musée Basque**. Anyone who wants to know something of the Basque people must go and spend as many hours as possible in it.

The museum is in a huge, square, massively built house with an open courtyard (now roofed in perspex) overhung with balconies. All floors are open and a wide display of Basque culture is on show. All seven provinces – Labourd, Bas-Navarre and Soule on the French side, Vizcaya, Guipuzcoa, Alava and Navarra on the Spanish – have their flags and costumes and coats of arms. There is much on the national sport of *pelota*, with all its variations. It looks a bit like squash, or real tennis, though you have to wear whites, shirt and trousers and a red sash. There is a *fronton*, a court with a high back wall and two lower side walls, and the players hurl the ball at the end wall and catch it on the rebound in basket-shapes on their hands called *chistera*, and hurl it back. There is a version called *main-nue*, bare hands without the basket, and an indoor game called *trinquet* or *paleta*, with a kind of bat. The museum has pelota equipment in all its forms, and pictures of past heroes. It also has rooms full of furniture; chocolate-making machinery with instructions; a loom; fishing boats for the whale and tuna, and their adventurous history (the Basque whaling fleet was operating off the coast of North America before Columbus blundered into it); and an array of agricultural implements. There is a chapel, typical gravestones, a goldsmith's shop, a basement room equipped as an inn with tables, fireplace, pots, bottles and gourds; and a dark, mysterious corner devoted to the cult of witchcraft, with paintings showing their devious works, all the witches depicted young and naked, with an actual broomstick for proof! There is a section of the museum devoted to such native writers and composers as Pierre Loti, who lived in Hendaye but wrote in the village of Ascain his celebrated work *Ramuntcho*, and Maurice Ravel. Although one of France's foremost composers of the early twentieth century, whose 'Daphnis and Chloe', for example, was rated highly avant-garde at the time, Ravel is most widely known outside France for his rhythmic, atavistic, haunting 'Bolero'. So much may be seen at the Musée Basque that there are probably recorded instances of Basque enthusiasts entering the museum and never coming out.

The museum tells all it can about the Basques and their way of life, past and present, but what it cannot do very simply is explain their origins and language, so I shall set out some of the arguments here.

Obscurity and mystery surround all discussions of this subject: learned professors, ethnologists, philologists and dozens of unlettered amateurs have exercized their minds and expended countless gallons of ink in the attempt to get at the solution. Everything from closely considered argument to wild and astonishing guesses have been put forward. The Basques themselves have hardly any written literature or history, but they do have a very strong oral tradition. But what they assert, say the professors, does not constitute evidence.

The speculation must begin with their language, Euskara, which is certainly very old and so difficult to learn that the Basques say it must be acquired from birth and even then it takes years. One nineteenth-century bishop proved that Adam and Eve spoke it, but the Basques themselves say this is unlikely: they have never had any trouble from the Devil because he has never been able to understand a word they say, therefore if Eve spoke Basque she and Adam would never have fallen.

Theories have ranged widely. Some have said that it is a dialect of Phoenician from some long-forgotten Phoenician colony, others that it is similar to Gaelic, Erse or Irish. Few scholars will commit themselves, as evidence is slight, but George Borrow, the nineteenth-century amateur philologist, commits himself as didactically as a saloon-bar bore. 'Much,' he says, 'that is vague, erroneous, and hypothetical has been said and written concerning this tongue. The Basques assert that it was not only the original language of Spain, but also of the world, and that from it all other languages are derived; but the Basques are a very ignorant people, and know nothing of the philosophy of language.'

Borrow dismisses the Phoenician theory as ridiculous. '... it were as unreasonable to suppose that the Basque is derived from it as that the Kamschatdale and Cherokee are dialects of the Greek or Latin.' He discusses the descent of such tongues as the Celtic dialect he calls Irish and concedes that it is derived from a dialect of Sanscrit – 'a remote one, as may well be supposed' – but when some of his contemporaries claim that Irish is similar to Basque, they are wrong: ' – perhaps in the whole of Europe it would be difficult to discover two languages which exhibit fewer points of resemblance than the Basque and Irish.'

So where does he think it does come from (and, therefore, the Basques themselves)? All the dialects of Europe, he says, may be traced back to two great Asiatic languages, Tibetan and Sanscrit: 'the Celtic, Gothic, and Sclavonian dialects in Europe belong to the Sanscrit family, even as in the East, the Persian, and to a lesser degree the Arabic, Hebrew, etc.; whilst to the Tibetan or Tartar family in Asia pertain the Mandchou and Mongolian, the Calmuc and the Turkish of the Caspian Sea, and in Europe the Hungarian and the Basque partially.'

Borrow admits that it is easier to say what Basque is not than what it is, but compares it with Tartar: 'Of these Tartar etymons I shall at present content myself with citing one, though, if necessary, it were easy to adduce hundreds. This word is Jauna, or as it is pronounced, Khauna, a word in constant use amongst the Basques, and which is the Khan of the Mongols and Mandchous, and of the same signification – Lord.'

If Borrow is right, then the Basques are Asiatic in origin. Science has produced an answer based on blood-grouping. The learned doctors Eyquem and Saint-Paul of the Pasteur Institute in Paris found that the Basques' blood types were 60 per cent O group and 27-35 per cent Rhesus negative, concluding thereby that the Basques 'represent the pure descendants of the people who occupied Europe in Paleolithic times and, throughout the continent, were crossed with Asian invaders.' They deduced also that the Basques' ancestors were the Franco-Cantabrians, so-called, whose civilization in the Old Stone Age stretched from Santander to the Dordogne. If this is right, then the Basques are justified in saying that they are the oldest inhabitants of Europe; and it might explain why some of their words are Asian in derivation.

It also might explain why Basque place-names occur on both

sides of the Pyrenees in areas where Basques have never been known to live. For example, Val d'Aran, the valley of the upper Garonne, is a Spanish extrusion into French territory. The people are not Basques, but the word Aran is Basque for valley. Before being re-named by the Romans the town of Elne, at the Mediterranean end of the Têt valley in the Roussillon, used to be called Illiberis, a Basque name. All over south-western France and much of Spain are places which have Basque-sounding names but no evidence of Basque habitation. In all other places save the Basque Country, the Basques were absorbed by other races, yet in that small north-western region of the Pyrenees they survived uncrossed and undiluted. Why did they survive? Perhaps the reason is geographical. They could exist on both sides of the mountains because there the passes were easy yet the valleys were deep and defensible. Intruders could be kept out and in any case their language defeated all attempts to incorporate them into surrounding political systems.

Although far from being typically Basque, Biarritz is a famous watering-place. Leave Bayonne on the N10, the coast road, for a quick look at its beach. Formidable Atlantic rollers thunder on the rocks framing 'la Plage', overlooked by the kind of hotels normally associated with places like Brighton. At one time, in the nineteenth century, when sea-side watering-places became universally popular, Biarritz attracted crowned and coroneted heads by the score, including the Emperor Napoleon III's. Even now it is fashionable, but has lost something of its old allure. Extricate yourself from its one-way system and continue along the coast, through Bidart and Guéthary, full of Basque-style villas in a variety of colours, making for **St-Jean-de-Luz**.

St-Jean, like Biarritz, has also acquired some modern hotels on the rim of the wide, spacious harbour, the two moles extending from each side like embracing arms, keeping out the ocean's winter fury. The old port is full of streets lined with ancient houses, all, whether in stone or timber-framed, of the Basque type: deep-eaved, gay with flowers in basket and balcony, all bearing a stone over the entrance carved with the family name and a date, many from the sixteenth and seventeenth centuries.

The town was built on a promontory on the east bank of the Nivelle estuary, enclosing a natural haven. The seaward side of the promontory was protected by the two moles, and modern buildings rise high above the quiet waters of the bay. There is, therefore, a slope down to the edge of the old harbour on the landward side, and the town's nucleus, Place Louis XIV. We lunched in Café Majestic on sandwiches filled with luscious Bayonne ham. M. le Patron did not look very Basque. The Basque type, we learned, was tall, thin, agile, with a long face, a prominent and bony nose, and dark or black hair. This fellow was short and fat; not, perhaps, to be wondered at because when we came in he was tucking into a sizeable feast, and we disturbed him. It was, however, a fine, well-appointed café, even though the prices were a bit steep for so early in the season.

We went to look at the harbour, which had quite a number of pleasure-boats as well as a few fishing-boats: it had that fishy, salty smell that makes the gulls scream and circle so attentively, as their ancestors must have done for hundreds of years in this place, for fishing fleets had been setting out from Donibane Loretzun, St-Jean's Basque name, since Noah pushed his Ark out.

The Basques sailed up the St Lawrence River, along the coasts of Labrador, Greenland and Hudson's Bay in the thirteenth and fourteenth centuries; their whaling fleet is attested to have been operating off Greenland in 1412; their navigators were famous: one piloted Columbus to the West Indies, another, Juan Sebastian Elcano, was Magellan's first mate and completed the first circumnavigation of the world when Magellan died.

Whales used to frequent the Bay of Biscay in the spring and autumnal equinoxes and St-Jean-de-Luz became the world's greatest, northern whaling port, its sailors earning all kinds of privileges from the Kings of France because of the oil they provided – mineral oil was still in the ground. By the end of the

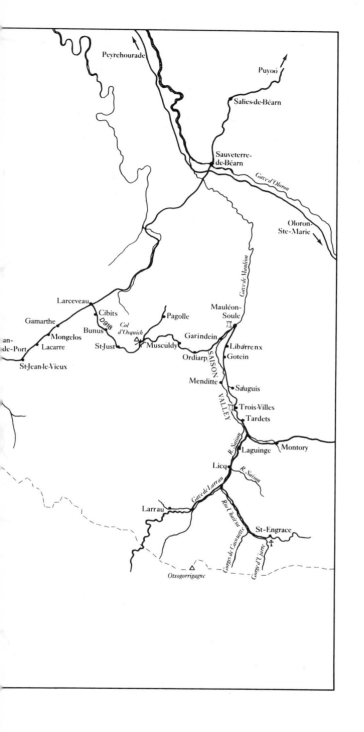

sixteenth century, the whaling fleet comprised nearly 100 ships of 200-300 tonnes each. Upwards of 3000 sailors left the port each spring to go whaling and cod-fishing, until at last the whales tumbled to what was happening, found somewhere else to go in the equinoxes and the fleet had to sail farther to find them. Other difficulties ensued. During the seventeenth and eighteenth centuries a series of devastating storms wrecked St-Jean's sea defences and flooded the town. More importantly, in 1713 the Treaty of Utrecht ceded their old fishing grounds off Canada and Newfoundland (which used to be called Port-au-Basques) to Britain, and St-Jean's prosperity was on the downward slope. From nearly 14,000 in 1730, the population had fallen by 1821 to 3500.

The Revolution was never popular in the south-west: the Convention changed St-Jean's name to Chauvin-le-Dragon, of all things; one may imagine that the Basques, as 'chauvinistic' as anyone, continued to call it Donibane Loretzun. When the Duke of Wellington and his army crossed the border they were welcomed as liberators from Napoleon's imperialism (they also paid for their board and lodging, which helped). Eventually the harbour was rebuilt over a long period in the nineteenth century; moles were projected from Socoa and Ste-Barbe, on either side of the bay, and another in the middle. The fishing industry began to pick up again with steam boats, and today they fish for tuna, sardine, and anchovy, depending on the time of year.

The church, of **St-Jean-Baptiste**, is big, almost windowless and formidable, like a castle. Inside are tiers of galleries and a huge altar-piece. On 9 June 1660 this was the scene of the wedding of King Louis XIV of France and the Infanta Marie-Thérèse, daughter of King Philip IV of Spain, and St-Jean-de-Luz has never forgotton the distinction. There is a café nearby still called 'Café Mariage de Louis XIV'.

Weddings usually take place in the church and reception rooms chosen by the bride's parents. If the bridegroom is a king, however, or the heir to a throne, he tends to call the tune. But

28

when the bride's father is a king too, what then? Two weddings, was the answer in 1660. First a ceremony on Spanish soil, in Fuenterrabia, just across the Bidassoa from Hendaye, at which the King of France was represented by a proxy. Then the bridal suite crossed the border and came to St-Jean-de-Luz.

The two finest houses in town were to accommodate the respective families and suites of France and Spain, and both were afterwards dignified by a name-change: Maison Haraneder became Maison de l'Infante, and the four-towered Maison Lohobiague was called Maison Louis XIV. The first was to be the bride's lodging: a beautiful Renaissance house on the quayside, in white stone and rose brick, two towers facing the waterfront. Through its classical portal came the splendidly arrayed bridal cortège in solemn procession, watched no doubt by the entire urban population, or at least the female section of it. The church was reached and the ceremony could begin, the king's party having already been installed. The king had entered the church by a side door, which afterwards was blocked up and has remained so ever since: once the king had passed through it, no lesser mortal should.

The wedding rites took three hours to complete: the bride wore, in addition to her heavy silver wedding-dress, a crown and a purple velvet cloak; it was early June, with the temperature in the customary seventies. One needs stamina to be a princess. The long liturgy, as incomprehensible for most in Basque as in Latin, no doubt, was over at last, and the procession, now swollen by the addition of the king's retinue, began the return to the Maison de l'Infante. From its balcony the king and his elderly Regent, Cardinal Mazarin, threw handfuls of commemorative medallions to the crowd. Then, once again, the wedding guests left the Maison de l'Infante and processed to the king's quarters in the Maison Louis XIV. Here dinner was served, and after many more hours the bridal couple were escorted upstairs; the Queen Mother, Anne of Austria, blessed them, drew the curtains round their bed, and left them at last to themselves.

The marriage was not a success, nor were its political developments. The new queen's half-brother, Charles X, married twice but had no heirs to the Spanish throne. When he died in 1700 Louis XIV at once claimed the throne for his grandson, Philip, and is said to have remarked, concerning the treaty of 1659 which had defined the border between France and Spain, *'Les Pyrenées n'existent plus.'* This was the possibility which alarmed other European powers, including Britain – that Spain and France might now unite, might one day come under a single crown and would certainly become overwhelmingly powerful, to the detriment of all others. The Austrians at once produced their own claimant to the Spanish throne, a grandson of Philip IV of Spain by his second, Austrian, wife; and in 1701 the long-lasting War of the Spanish Succession began.

During the revolutionary period the Place Louis XIV also changed its name and a guillotine was set up outside the Town Hall. It used to be possible to see the words 'Place de la Liberté' on the wall of Maison Louis XIV, but we failed to find them, though we did find the oldest house in the town, a sixteenth-century stone house with a tower, at 2 Rue de la Republique. The tourist trade has come to the rescue of the fishing fleet, and St-Jean's population is currently around 17,000. The majority of them, no doubt, fish for profits from the visitors rather than the sea.

A bridge over the Nivelle leads to the village of **Ciboure**, adjacent to but independent of St-Jean-de-Luz. Its name in Basque means 'head of the bridge' and its history, too, is fishy: the stout houses along the quayside are built, as it were, on scaly backs. In one of them was born Maurice Ravel, and the whole quayside is named after him. Our reference said that his house was No 12 but we could find no No 12, as they were all odd numbers. Puzzled, we searched up a back-street in case the even numbers were in the rear, but found nothing. Coming round to the quayside again we solved the mystery: the numbers had been changed. No 27 was tall, red-stoned, balconied and apparently permanently closed up, but it did have an old No 12 inscribed on it and furthermore a plaque that said: 'Dans cette maison est né Maurice Ravel, le 7 Mars 1875.'

There used to be a separate race of people all along the Pyrenees, called Cagots. They were outcasts, untouchables, who lived alone, and having no lands to cultivate, practised the trades of wood-cutter, mason or weaver. A community of them used to live in Ciboure. Other Pyreneans were not permitted to marry them, or have any more to do with them than was absolutely necessary. They were probably descended from a colony of lepers.

Cross the bridge again and take the road following the Nivelle upstream, into the gentle, green Labourdais countryside. At **Ascain**, cross the Nivelle and head uphill to La Rhune, the most westerly of the Pyrenean peaks on the French side. It is very small compared with others, at about 2950 feet, and its grassy slopes have evidently been used for cattle-grazing – its name is a corruption of the Basque 'Larre-on', meaning good moorland. Ascain is a picture-postcard of a place, the archetypal Basque village, so near to the hotels of St-Jean-de-Luz and Biarritz that it is flooded with tourists in the season. By the fronton, the pelota court, is the hotel where Pierre Loti, who normally lived in Hendaye, wrote one of his books, called *Ramuntcho*.

A miniature pass called Col de St-Ignace skirts La Rhune, which, as J. B. Morton put it in *The Pyrenean*, 'squatted like a great animal . . . it is a hideous mountain when you get close to it'. Despite its modest height, La Rhune was covered in snow on our visit, which gave a certain validity to Morton's opprobrium. In Sare we stopped for a while. Like Ascain, it is almost too perfect, too neat, well-kept and tidy; in the square the old stone houses face the church, whose clock chimed three in the stillness of the afternoon. The spacious *fronton* had stone terraces on either side, like a Roman theatre.

Crossing the meandering Nivelle again we went by diverse

ways through the shining, green, prosperous Basque farmland to **Espelette**. Again typically Basque in its architecture, Espelette is not quite so obviously in the 'best-kept village' category and is therefore more authentic. Oddly enough, it did twice win the title 'Prettiest Village of France' but the last time was in 1955 and since then it seems to have subsided into a more comfortable untidiness. A feature, as in St-Jean, of some of its timber-framed old houses, jettied, deep-eaved and curly-tiled, is the symbol called the 'Lauburu', carved on the lintels, over the door, along with the date of building and the name of the family. It is a kind of feminine swastika, with curves instead of sharp angles, another of the ancient European sun-wheel symbols from the pagan past.

It is a short distance from Espelette to **Cambo-les-Bains**, one of the many thermal stations in the Pyrenees and a good centre for visiting the Basque region. The efficacy of the sulphurous waters springing from many parts of the mountains was known to the Romans, and is still bringing help to many, whether taken externally or internally. The old town of Cambo, as Basque as any, sits on the ridge overlooking the Nive on its way to Bayonne: spread out behind it is the nineteenth-century development, large and splendid villas, in Thermal Station Rococo style, which have mostly been converted into hotels or sanatoria.

We went shopping in this new part of Cambo. There were souvenir shops, selling the usual range of tasteless rubbish, and there was also a good drapery. 'Linge Basque' is the approved colour and pattern, but when we selected a table-cloth we found there were not enough napkins of the same kind to go with it. The shop was run by a couple who had emigrated from Paris, having tired of the urban rat-race, and Madame volunteered to run up a few more napkins for us. It would take *'un quart d'heure'*. 'Linge Basque' is any kind of article in the style of Basque linen, which is coloured in red, green or blue and patterned in white, in a distinctive fashion.

We walked downhill, towards the river, in search of the Bath-house. Though we failed to find it, we did pass many of the grandiose villas which people used to rent for a season at the waters. In one at the other side of the town lived Edmond Rostand, the writer who in 1897 produced a story about a poet-adventurer with an exceptionally long nose, Cyrano de Bergerac.

Our napkins completed, the whole purchase carefully wrapped, we asked if the Porte de Maya was clear of snow, but the couple had only been in Cambo a short while and had not even heard of Maya. We returned through Espelette and on down through Ainhoa to the twin border villages of Dancharia and Dancharinea, where the frontier guards and customs men of France and Spain waved us through.

A road leading off from the border posts goes to Zugarramurdi, a village sheltering under the summit of a mountain called Aizchuri, 2,500 feet, not far south-east of La Rhune. This summit was the gathering-place for witches, called Sorgiñak, those sexy temptresses depicted so mysteriously in Bayonne's Musée Basque. They continued as a cult in the Basque Country, despite Christian influence, with a secret organization and fertility rites, until at least the seventeenth century, giving rise to a specifically Basque vocabulary: 'Jaun Gori' was the Red Lord, and 'akelare' was the witches' sabbath. The terms and customs and beliefs are not closely paralleled outside the Basque Country, and probably represent a survival, in a very old race of people, of an ancient pagan religion.

The road twisted up to the Porte de Maya, called in Basque 'Otxondo', and although in March there was plenty of snow about, the road was clear: a quick succession of hairpin bends, up to the pass and down from it. We passed through many small villages, and noticed that although these houses on the Spanish side of the mountains were in the same unmistakable Basque style as on the French side, they seemed more decrepit, poorer, less fresh-painted and cared-for.

The road descended along the valley of the Baztan (Rat's tail) and arrived in Elizondo. This was the second time I had been here, and on both occasions it rained, which is a pity, because Elizondo is a very pretty place. I had once stayed in the Hotel

Trinquete-Anchitonea, a typically massively built, Basque-featured structure facing towards the river. Attached to it, and its name, was a *trinquet* court and there I had watched the semi-finals of the local *paleta* championship: the court was deep and long, with a spectators' gallery high along one side. The game was played with a flat wooden bat and a hard rubber ball, like a squash ball. It was a doubles match, two forward, two back: the ball was served against the end wall, and players of alternate sides had to play it on the rebound. It could bounce off any of the forward three walls, the roof, or the spectators, as long as it was still in play. Once it could no longer be played by any player, points were scored which ran into games, sets and match. The speed was astonishing, and the players I saw – a local side who were probably not in the same league as the real experts – displayed lightning reflexes, supple and athletic agility and sheer beefy strength, since of course the harder you hit the ball, the faster it goes. Some of the saves and returns seemed like a fairground bullet-catcher's act, and they had the spectators ooh-ing and aah-ing, shouting and cheering.

We were now over the Pyrenees and heading for Pamplona, capital of Navarra, one of the Spanish Basque provinces and virtually of all the Spanish Basques. It is worth visiting at any time, but is at its colourful best in early July, when the fiesta of San Fermin turns the whole city into a holiday carnival. Accommodation is at a premium, and needs to be booked early in the year.

To reach Pamplona there was more climbing to do. The Baztan goes west to join the Bidassoa, becoming the frontier between Spain and France, and the road climbs over one of those lateral ridges so typical of the Spanish Pyrenees. Up and up, winding slowly, to the Puerto de Velate and down the long road to Pamplona, picking up first the Mediano and then the Ulzama rivers and following them. The scenery becomes dramatically savage, with great rocky chasms; then, in the river-valleys lower down, smoother and more pastoral.

Farther down the Bidassoa valley, there is an interesting connection with its function as border. In the middle of the River Bidassoa between Hendaye on the French side and Irun on the Spanish, is an island, called the **Isle of Pheasants**. It is quite small and completely undistinguished except that it has figured in no fewer than four international transactions between the two neighbouring states. The first occurred in 1526, after King François I of France had been thoroughly beaten at the battle of Pavia, in Italy, by the Emperor Charles V. These two monarchs, along with England's Henry VIII, for many years indulged in a complicated *danse-à-trois*, each playing one off against the others. Their vanity and ambition did nothing to pacify a Europe at the start of the massive and cataclysmic turbulence caused by the refusal of the Church to reform itself, and the impatience of those who insisted that it should.

The battle of Pavia in the year before had ended with the capture of François I. The victorious Emperor was willing to release him but only if his two children were given as surety, and the exchange took place on the little island. The next handover was much more amicable. In 1615, King Louis XIII of France received his fiancée, Anne of Austria, daughter of Philip III of Spain, and presented his sister Elizabeth as fiancée for his brother-in-law, later Philip IV.

Forty-four years later, in 1659, the island was used to draw up and sign the Treaty of the Pyrenees, which marked out and laid down the frontier between France and Spain for ever and ever (with a good many twists and cheats, which will be good for a sardonic smile later on). The island for a time was known as Ile de la Conférence as a result. Lastly, in 1856, another 'Frontiers' treaty laid down that the island should be governed alternately by a Spanish viceroy, the first half of every year, then by a French one for the second half. The French viceroy was usually the commanding officer of their naval base of the Bidassoa; but as the island is only 118 yards by 13, and no one lives there, it really doesn't matter very much.

Having crossed the Arga, Pamplona's river, we entered the city by the road that climbs quickly up to the ridge on which it was built, along Avenida Baja Navarra. When we arrived it was the rush-hour and we didn't know where to park. Had we continued along the same road for another couple of hundred yards, we would have found plenty of parking space, but not knowing that we turned off at one of the roundabouts and started to go slightly frantic. The traffic obeyed no known rules of the road, pedestrians were clearly totally demented, and by the end of five minutes so were we. At last we saw a big 'P' sign and counted ourselves lucky to find what appeared to be the last space in the Plaza de Toros which fringed the looming mass of the bullring.

# 2

# Pamplona and Roncesvalles

ONGI ETORRIAK: Irunean, Sanferminetan, ez dago atzerri-
tarrarik. Zure buruarentzat eskatzen duzun errespetoaz egoten
bezara jendearekin, ez zara atzerritarra izanen.

The above message is in Basque, and embodies the essence of
what is expected of crowd behaviour at the festival of San Fermin.
'Welcome', it says. 'During San Fermin there are no outsiders in
Pamplona. If you behave as you would at home, you will certainly
not be made to feel one.' The festival has taken place on the
saint's day, 7 July, since 1591, and extends over seven days. San
Fermin himself is not prominent in the Church's hagiography,
and was not even a bishop of Pamplona. He was, however, a
native, and was converted by St Saturninus in the third century.
His name was actually Firminus, and in due course he became the
first Bishop of Amiens, in northern France: his saint's day there is
25 September. His festival is far better known, indeed its
celebration is world-famous. Even our attempt to book July
accommodation in March turned out to be impossible, so in the
end I went on my own, with a small pack containing my old tent, a
plastic groundsheet and an Arab blanket bought in Tunis more
than twenty years before.

I arrived by air from Heathrow and touched down at Bilbao in
late afternoon on Sunday, 5 July. Enquiries had failed to reveal

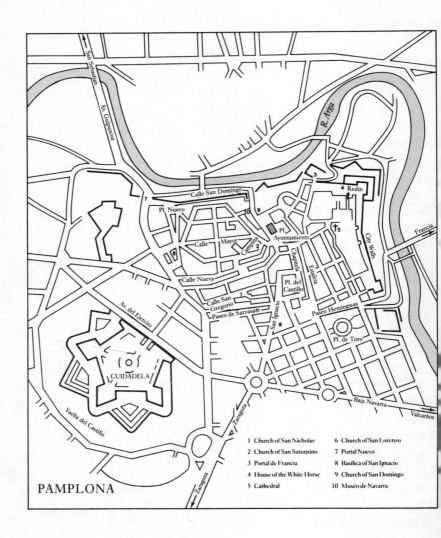

PAMPLONA

1 Church of San Nicholas    6 Church of San Lorenzo
2 Church of San Saturnino    7 Portal Nuevo
3 Portal de Francia    8 Basilica of San Ignacio
4 House of the White Horse    9 Church of San Domingo
5 Cathedral    10 Muséo de Navarra

any convenient trains from Bilbao to Pamplona (there is no direct line between the two cities) and no one, not even the Spanish Tourist Office in London, had any information about coaches or buses. The young lady at Bilbao's airport information desk wrote on a piece of paper the name of the street the bus station was in, and advised me to take a taxi. Two others, in similar straits, wished to share it, and at the bus station we encountered a third: the four of us crammed into a taxi whose driver was willing to take us all the way to Pamplona. Shared between four, the fare was still three times more than the bus fare, as I discovered later. A motorway ran directly to Pamplona, and soon we were hurtling along it, through some wild, rocky, spectacular scenery. Three of us wished to locate the official camping site, so another taxi took us there, out on the far side of Pamplona, along Avenida Baja Navarra, across the Arga and along the road towards the Pass of Maya. The site was at least three miles out of town, which would be difficult to negotiate each day. It was on a hillside on the right bank of the Ulzama, near a village called Oricain, and it was seething with people, caravans, tents, cars and bicycles: there would be no room, now or in the foreseeable future, said the young lady in the booking-in office, for even a very small tent.

Eventually, after buying bread and salami in the village shop and beer in the overcrowded bar, I made camp down by the river-side, where there was plenty of grassy space, the clear river-water for ablutions, and where many others had already established themselves.

Heavy rain fell that evening, and the morning was overcast still. Buses ran from Oricain to Pamplona, but infrequently, so I decided to strike camp, load up and walk in; perhaps I could camp nearer to the centre of things that night. Thin cloud screened the sun, but the morning was warm and the pastoral Ulzama valley enjoyable. Near its end the road dropped away to the Arga plain and across it I could see Pamplona, on its craggy clifftop.

A defensible site like this was an obvious attraction for people wishing for security against allcomers. The Basque name for it is

Iruña. No doubt they called it that before the Romans came building roads, but as in all probability the Romans never did understand Euskarra, they called it Pompaelo. It was their road which crossed the mountains by the Pass of Roncesvalles, from Burdigala, the Roman name for Bordeaux, and from Pompaelo it struck westward across northern Spain, just one section of the network of roads that made the province of Hispania governable. Pamplona's hill is 1485 feet above sea level, with a sheer drop down to the Arga. On the other side it is defended by a series of fortifications: the hill subsides into a plateau, sloping towards the next river-system.

Having climbed up the road skirting the clifftop, I made for the Plaza del Castillo, Pamplona's principal square, which has an abundance of trees in its centre and arcaded hotels, shops and cafés on all sides, with tables and chairs spilling out over the pavement into the road. By this time it was mid-morning. Many people were about in the city's streets, the majority of them young and dressed identically. During the week of the Sanfermines, one wears white: white shirt, white trousers (or skirt for the ladies, or a white dress) and white shoes. Around the waist is tied a red sash, around the neck, a red scarf.

The scarf is the essential part of this costume, for Pamplonese, neighbouring Navarrese, and for any visitor, like myself. Essential because the tradition is that 'as long as we retain the first red kerchief we wore at Sanfermines, so long are we sure of returning some other July to Pamplona'. Some are patterned, like the one I bought in the street market in Paseo Sarasate, with a flag of Navarre (which acts as the flag of the Basques) – red, with a white cross superimposed on a green saltire; some bear the coat of arms of Pamplona – a lion, with a crown over it; some the words 'Siete de julio, San Fermin'.

On the far side of the square was a bus acting as information centre. I was given a city map and a news-sheet displaying (in Spanish) the time-table of events for the whole week. Having discovered that one could leave luggage at the bus station, I did so, and there was now nothing else to do but join the swelling crowds and prepare to enjoy the festival. By the side of Paseo Sarasate, a wide, open thoroughfare with a paved walk down the middle for the street-traders' stalls, stood the Church of San Nicolas, a stoutly built, semi-fortified building of the early thirteenth century, on the site of an earlier, romanesque basilica. A service was in progress, even now, at nearly 11.30 on 6 July: at noon, the Fiesta of San Fermin was to be officially opened, and the air of expectancy was hotting up.

Through the narrow, crowded streets, decked out with flags and balloons, I walked slowly, moving with the mass; there was a consistent surge in one direction, so I went along with it. At the end of a street, Calle Nueva, a throng of white-and-red merrymakers were packed tightly together, many of them in possession of bottles of champagne. I squeezed into a position near the corner and waited. This was Plaza Consistorial, also known as Plaza del Ayuntamiento. At the end of the little square was the town hall, the Ayuntamiento, a wonderfully baroque façade, balconied, ornamented with carvings and statuary, and at present smothered in people. In front of it, in the square, was a scaffolding platform, also swarming with bodies, clinging on by their fingers, toes and teeth. All around, the tall houses reared up, spectators at every window and on every balcony, some even on the rooftops, and one hardy soul perched on the very chimney-top with his camera. In the square the closely-packed crowd surged and swayed, drenched by sprays of champagne fizz on all the crowd. Balloons floated above the crowd, kept airborne by constant pushes, dodged by the diving swallows, tiny black shapes against the bright sky. The crush could have been frightening but good humour and tolerance, the hallmark of Sanfermines, were already evident: the people were there to enjoy themselves. They were singing and chanting. Periodically they would end a song and begin to chant, holding their red scarves above their heads. 'San Fermin, San Fermin, San Fermin!' The songs were various, but one of them was the traditional theme-song of the Fiesta:

# The Pyrenees

Uno de enero, dos de febrero,
Tres de marzo, cuatro abril,
Cinco de mayo, seis de junio,
Siete de julio, San Fermin.
A Pamplona hemos de irnos,
Con una media, con una media,
A Pamplona hemos de irnos,
Con una media y un calcetin.

At last the hands on the town hall clock are nearly together. The shouting and chanting intensifies, the noise is tremendous. Then the doors of the lower balcony open to emit some gentlemen in feathered cocked hats, who beat drums and blow trumpets. Then, on the upper balcony, the mayor announces briefly on the public address that the Fiesta is open, and at once lets off the first of a series of rockets. The crowd goes wild. Sanfermines of 1987 has begun. All around the people are dancing, hugging and kissing each other, pouring champagne down their throats (the gutters are ten deep in empties, but the municipal dustmen get going very promptly). The atmosphere is overwhelmingly joyful, as if some great liberating victory had been won.

The band in red berets and white-and-red Sanfermines dress, which has been standing patiently by the town hall throughout, now strike up and march off, slowly because of the press, along the Calle Mayor. Dodging the spurting champagne-fizz and the pails-ful of water periodically thrown on the sweating crowd from balconies, I left the Plaza, round the corner to Calle Campana, and slipped into the Church of San Saturnino. It was cool and quiet, and I needed to give my eardrums and my entire equilibrium respite from the percussive battering of the last half-hour.

San Saturnino, or San Cernin, is an early fourteenth-century Gothic church, but it has a north door which displays thirteenth-century polychrome work in its capitals. It also has two towers and a good deal of machicolation and other defence-work, so that from the outside it looks more like a castle. The interior

42

has been renewed in Renaissance style, with a cupola. San Cernin or Saturninus was a missionary from Rome who evangelized the district around Pamplona and then the territory and city of Toulouse, where he became its first bishop. He is said to have been martyred in the persecution of Valerian, in 257, by being fastened behind a wild bull, which dragged him about until he was dashed to pieces. Emerging again into brightness and colour and din, I made my way slowly through the singing crowd round the rear of the town hall to the municipal covered market, making for the gate in the city wall called variously Portal de Francia and Portal de Zumalacarregui, then up the tree-lined walk inside the wall where others were seeking a little peace. At the top of the slight rise a bastion of the old defences has been laid out as a public belvedere, where one may sit and enjoy the view over the Arga plain. Close by is a building called the House of the White Horse, a much-restored fifteenth-century Gothic cottage incorporated into a bastion of the walls, and now a restaurant. Turning abruptly by this corner, the street returns to the close-packed houses of the old town, under a covered passage connecting the houses' upper storeys on either side. Round the next corner the street, Calle Redin, emerges into Plaza San José, before the cathedral.

This is the highest end of the city, the site of the capitol of Roman Pompaelo. Successive cathedrals have stood on this spot, ever since the first bishop of Pamplona was enthroned, when there were very few other bishops in the whole of northern Spain; one cathedral, in the romanesque style, is known to have been consecrated in 1124. A new cloister was begun in 1317, but part of the cathedral collapsed in 1390; rebuilding began in 1397 when King Charles III, 'the Noble', of Navarre, laid the foundation stone. In the centre of the nave a splendid tomb was built for him and his wife, Doña Leonor, designed by Jean Lomme of Tournai. Rebuilding went on right through the fifteenth century, and was not completed until 1525, but parts of the original romanesque fabric are still visible. The façade, with its twin towers, was superimposed in the eighteenth century by Ventura Rodriguez, in a neo-classical style; the northern tower of the two accommodates a bell of 1584, at 12,000 kilos the second largest in Spain. The north door of the cathedral, called Puerta de San José, belongs to the fifteenth-century rebuilding, and still has its original wooden doors. The choir-stalls are contemporary with the great bell, carved by Obray; they are not easy to see, since there are no windows below the clerestory. On the high altar is a much venerated statue of the Virgin Mary known variously as La Virgen del Sagrario or Santa Maria del Real, before which the Kings of Navarre used to be crowned; the last was in 1572, so this is indeed an antiquity.

There is only a small space in front of the cathedral and the streets running down from it are narrow, so there is no clear view of it. It occurred to me that no one had recently viewed it with municipal pride, because small shrubs were growing out of the stonework of the towers, and vegetation was visible elsewhere among the masonry.

During San Fermin, one drinks, naturally, but one also eats whenever possible in order to stay, however unsteadily, on one's feet. The Pamplona news-sheet advises the Sanfermines reveller to 'eat as much and as greedily as you can in order to survive the effort and delight of the Fiesta'. There was an upstairs restaurant of a small hotel in Calle San Gregorio, where the proprietor, in white shirt and red scarf, scurried about happily, making himself audible above the cheering and shouting and band-playing in the street below his open windows, and he served me an excellent lunch of paella, grilled ham, ice-cream and good red wine, very cheaply. Afterwards I turned from the end of San Gregorio into Taconera, past the church of San Lorenzo with its chapel of San Fermin, both inexplicably closed, and strolled on down under the bridged city wall called Portal Nuevo, to Avenida Guipuzcoa along the riverside.

The afternoon is the time when Sanfermines revellers sleep off the effects of the morning's celebrations, and the city streets are consequently quieter for visitors with sufficient stamina for sight-seeing. For example, if they can tear themselves away from the cafés in Plaza del Castillo (one of which, Café Iruña, features in Hemingway's *The Sun Also Rises*), they might go to the south side of the square, past the Government buildings, to the **Basilica of San Ignacio**, built on the spot where St Ignatius Loyola, founder of the Jesuits, was wounded in 1521; the basilica was opened in 1624. Or, going north from the Plaza, past the Ayuntamiento, they could see the church of San Domingo, a late Gothic church of the sixteenth century with a renaissance reredos and some ancient tombs. Farther along Calle San Domingo, hard by the city walls, there is the **Museo de Navarra**, in what once was a hospital building, with a façade dating from 1556. The museum has relics of Pamplona's past, from pre-historic times, through the centuries of Roman occupation, to examples of mediaeval art such as some magnificent murals; and items of fascination like an Arabic ivory chest which used to belong to the monastery of Leyre, and a Goya portrait of the Marques de San Adrian.

That night I found a tolerable camp-site in a field I had spotted on my way into town. It was not too level, but to compensate for its deficiencies, a short walk in the morning would bring me to Plaza de Toros. I woke and struck camp early. Sleep, in fact, had been hard to come by because the traffic never stopped, and neither until very late did the music from a party somewhere adjacent: San Fermin had begun.

Today was the 7th, Siete de Julio, and I wanted to see the **Encierro**, the running of the bulls through the streets. I was in town by 7.20 am and already a huge multitude thronged the streets and the barricades, which workmen were trying, in face of great difficulties from the swelling crowds, to complete. I stood at the barricade at the end of Paseo Hemingway, near the bullring, where the runners would eventually arrive and dash off in one direction, and the bulls would be diverted in another, into the ring.

No one knows when the tradition of the bull-running started, but it goes on every morning of the seven days of Sanfermines. The bulls are corralled near the Portal de Rochapea, and at eight o'clock precisely, two rockets are let off. This is the signal that the bulls have been loosed: six bulls, followed by six steers. The course is less than half a mile – along Santo Domingo, across the Plaza Consistorial, around Mercaderes and into Estafeta. It is the privilege of the lads to run before the bulls, and run hard they must, because the bulls are fleet of foot and very heavy. 'La curva de la Calle Estafeta es peligrosa' says the Pamplona news-sheet, and most years there are casualties. In addition to the white-and-red-clad Navarrese boys, there is always nowadays a large contingent of foreigners, many of whom have not sobered up from the night before and can scarcely stand, let alone run. In fact, considering the dangers, the bill of mortality is surprisingly low: twelve have been killed since 1924, although in 1980 one bull killed two men in a morning.

It is done for the sake of deliberately running the risk of death, a specifically Spanish conception. *Macho* and *bravado*, both Spanish words, signify the Spaniard's willingness to risk his life for the sake of a reputation. His manliness depends upon it, so he does it.

Standing as I did in the crowd behind the barrier, I could see little. On tip-toe, craning above the equally interested person in front, I could see the runners, hundreds of them, then at once the brown and white of the bulls' backs and the steers, and it was all over. The barriers were lifted, the crowds began to move away; so did the Red Cross men, with one on a stretcher who had not run as fast as the bulls.

A huge number of outside visitors were now in town. In all the parks and open spaces, even on the dirty verges of car parks, there were recumbent shapes draped in sleeping bags. Necessity had obliged me to dispense with the niceties of ablutions for a night or two: these people looked as though they had forgone such pleasures for weeks at a stretch.

I went shopping in the street-market again, making my way

back through Plaza del Castillo and up Chapitela to watch the 7 July procession. At 10 am every 7 July it leaves the town hall, goes to the cathedral, where it is joined by the archbishop and chapter, then they all make their way, bands playing, to the Church of San Lorenzo to collect the highly decorated, mitred image of San Fermin from his chapel. The procession weaves its way through the streets of the old town, led by several giant figures called Gigantes, at least nine feet tall, grotesques in the form of Moors or Saracens from Spain's Moslem past and old favourites of the Sanfermines crowds. Bands, dancers, the mayor and corporation of the city with mace-bearers and the trumpeting gentlemen in cocked hats are followed by the banners and crosses of the five parishes of Pamplona, then the cathedral clergy in all their lace finery, and the archbishop himself in his glowing purple cope. The churchmen are escorted by a bodyguard of resplendent characters in blue-and-white uniforms with high shiny boots and white-plumed helmets, and then comes the town band, the Pamplonesa, playing traditional, cheerful, but stately marching tunes. At various points along the route they pause for the dancing of a *jota* or *gaita*, or the parading, cavorting and dancing of the Gigantes, to the delight of onlookers. It is a wonderfully colourful, happy and endearing spectacle.

From 6 July, every day until the end of the fiesta, including the 14th, there is a *corrida*, a bullfight, at 6.30 pm. Tickets for these are hard to come by as 90 per cent are season tickets, sold long beforehand. The remaining 10 per cent require hours spent waiting at the box-office. Posters are displayed announcing the names of the three *toreros*, bullfighters, of the day, and the name of the breeder of the bulls. The public always wants to know where the bulls come from, so that they will be able to gauge their fighting spirit: a limp and spiritless bull will give no entertainment.

At 5.30 pm every day during the fiesta, the bullfighters and their assistants, all in their colourful dress, leave the town hall accompanied by a band, and march across Plaza del Castillo on their way to the bullring. Simultaneously, bands of supporters, grouped into factions called *peñas*, also process to the arena and take their seats. Every bullring is in two sections: the sun and the shade. The shade is for the older, more astute and knowledgeable spectators, the sun for the *peñas*, who sing, drink and dance. When the third bull of the evening is killed, they begin a gargantuan feast. It is a party atmosphere, but intense, emotional; the *peñas* are also a cloak for political activity, and their songs may be jibes at the police or the government.

Bullfighting is not a sport and no one pretends that it is. It is more like a national ritual – the *aficionados* claim it is an art-form, since a skilled *torero* will take on a spirited bull and perform, with his graceful movements, his feints and his thrusts, something akin to a ballet. The expert *torero* will maintain his reputation by aiming always for the perfect kill, the thrust straight into the bull's heart. He is also risking his life in that fatalistic Spanish way: many a matador has been killed by the bull: Francesco Paquirri died in 1984, and in 1985 twenty-year-old José Yiyoé was killed.

The Spanish do not call it 'fighting'; they have their own vocabulary. The base word is *toro*, the bull. *Torear* is the verb, *torero* the man. The word *matador* means killer, and *gran matador de toros* is one of the élite, a highly paid star of the bullring. The best explanation of the phenomenon I have read is Hemingway's, in his book *The Sun Also Rises*, also published under the name *Fiesta*. It is not a particularly good book, but it does contain a vivid description of the San Fermin fiesta, and Hemingway himself always returned every year.

There is a very full programme, every day, in all parts of Pamplona, of dancing displays, bands playing, processions; and every night at 11 pm a prodigious firework display from the gardens in the citadel. The citadel is a complicated military fortress in the south-west of the city, with sharp angles, moats, redoubts and every sophistication of the style of the great Vauban, though it is not of his design. One old gun remains, outside what looks like the former officers' mess, but all the rest is grass-grown, generally a quiet, pleasant retreat full of wild birds and insects, bees and butterflies.

Sanfermines, throughout its whole week, it not simply a festival of bull-killing, nor is it an orgy of unlicensed drinking. It can be whole-heartedly enjoyed without ever seeing a bull and, especially by children, without ever tasting alcohol. There is so much going on, so much colour and vivacity, so much sheer light-hearted enjoyment. They say that when the fiesta ends, at midnight on the 14th, people go again to the Plaza del Ayuntamiento with candles, in mourning, and chant a kind of dirge, '*Pobre de mi y traca*', with tears in their eyes; for it is all over for another year. I have kept my red San Fermin scarf.

Pamplona is the capital of the ancient Kingdom of Navarre, which straddled the Pyrenees. To reach the French part of it you need to use the famous Pass of Roncesvalles, then continue your gradual eastern progress from Navarre into the Basque province of Soule, nestling in the foothills of the spectacular northern side of the mountains.

Once on the Valcarlos road we were soon out of the city, through its suburb, Huarte, and following the brown Arga through the Basque villages of Anchoriz, Larrasoaña, Urdañiz and Zubiri, gradually rising above the plain. The landscape was still pastoral, but the hills were a confused jumble. Houses in the villages were uniformly Basque in character and style, but neglected, dejected, needy, missing the smug opulence of those on the French side of the mountains. At Zubiri we left the rushing Arga and started to climb, zig-zag, to a minor pass called Alto Erro, then down to Erro village, strung out along the side of the mountain above the Erro river. Much cautious negotiation of hairpin-bending roads followed, among pine-clad hillsides and a few more scattered small villages like Espinal. The road we had been following, C135, now met the valley road of Valle de Arce in the form of a T-junction, and we turned left, entering at last a long straight stretch for a change. Burguete was a line of white, deep-eaved houses, high in the hills at 2,900 feet. Summer visitors come here from the cities in the plains, enjoying the cool breeze that often blows and, like Hemingway's heroes, revelling in the opportunities for fishing in the nearby Irati. The Irati valley is called Aezcoa in Basque, a deeply forested, beautiful and sparsely populated region worth seeing whether for piscatorial purposes or not.

A short climb from Burguete brought us to an inn, a tiny chapel, and beyond it the shadowy shape of the monastery of **Roncesvalles**. The church, with a zinc roof, was founded as a staging post for pilgrims going to Compostela, by King Sancho the Strong of Navarre, in the thirteenth century. The little group of forlorn buildings stands a little way below the pass the Basques call Ibañeta, the French Roncevaux, and the rest of the world Roncesvalles.

Ibañeta, at 3,468 feet, was known to and used by the Basques from time immemorial. The Romans incorporated it into their road system linking Gallia and Hispania, calling it Imus Pyrenaeus, thereby creating a permanent thoroughfare. During the seventh century, Christian Spain was invaded and conquered by the Saracens, or Moors, from Africa, in the course of their Holy War for the forcible imposition of Islam on the world. They carried their war into France, too, until the victory of Charles Martel at Poitiers in 732 stopped them. In 777 his grandson, Charles the Great (Charlemagne) King of the Franks, was approached by one Sulaiman ben Alarabi, Governor of Barcelona, to assist him in a conspiracy against his master the Caliph, Abd-ar-Rahman. Charlemagne, clearly, would have done nothing without some inducement: the deal must have had something in it for him. In all probability he saw it as an opportunity to afford some relief to the hard-pressed Christians of Spain and at the same time to strengthen his southern frontier, the Spanish March. In 778 Charlemagne took a large army and crossed by Roncesvalles. In Pamplona, the Basque capital of Navarre, he consulted its inhabitants (with difficulty, no doubt, because of the language) and learned that his ally Sulaiman had captured Zaragoza.

The Basques were uncertain allies: in their fierce independence they were accustomed to fighting anyone indiscriminately, whether Moors, Franks or Asturians, who threatened them. Charlemagne accordingly marched his army to Zaragoza, but found that it had been taken by another Saracen chief, hostile to his cause. He did nothing about this, instead ravaging the countryside and looting the fortress towns of Huesca, Barcelona and Gerona, both to occupy his men and give them the profit of booty for which they had come, and also to remove the danger these strongholds presented to the mountain approaches and his own frontiers.

He then returned to Pamplona, having achieved nothing very substantial, and made the first of two crucial mistakes. Charlemagne considered Pamplona too isolated an outpost effectively to hold against the Moors and so he destroyed its defences in order that the Moors might not use them. Next, he divided his army, leading the march back to France himself with the main fighting force and leaving the baggage-train to follow, under the command of Count Roland of the Breton Marches.

Having infuriated the Basques by depriving them of the means to defend themselves in their capital, and then leaving his baggage-train, heavily laden with plundered riches, to make its ponderous way over the mountains under an inadequate guard, Charlemagne was either under-estimating the Basques' depth of animosity against him, and over-rating Roland's ability to withstand it, or he was completely off his trolley. In either case, ordinary prudence was not conspicuous.

Slowly the column toiled up the slopes of the hills, through the great beech wood and on to the col of Roncesvalles. As they reached it, they could pause and look ahead to their homeland. 'Here was a prodigious cleft,' writes Hilaire Belloc, 'running dead north, thousands of feet sunk sheer into the earth, and slowly widening its sides to where, far away at the opening of it in the

51

misty distance, in the V-shaped mouth of the hills, like a calm sea in misty weather, lay the Gascon plains.'

The great ox-drawn wagons lumbered up the road, over the col, down the zig-zags of the precipitous northern side, men, beasts, horses, wagons, siege-machines, all filing slowly, laboriously by. Count Roland eyed the green hillsides, now darkened by the deserting sun, shadowy and mysterious:

> High are the hills, the valley dark and deep,
> Grisly the rocks, and wondrous grim the steeps.

Darkness falls, the eery stillness deepens. The escort guards, watching anxiously, think they see the bushes move, that they in turn are being watched. A deathly chill creeps into the hearts of the Franks, a dreadful apprehension. They glance quickly over their shoulders, march faster, urge on the tired beasts, try to move closer to those distant plains. 'In that profound ravine there was no noise at all except the running of the torrent in the forest below. The walls were very steep, so steep that in places the beech-trees had lost their hold and had fallen down the precipitous earth; and perilously along the front of that slope went the road.'

Suddenly a massive boulder comes crashing down from a great height, smashing its way across the crowded road, down to the abyss, and simultaneously the air is filled with hideous, unearthly shrieks that freeze the mind and bring babbled prayers to lips. A human avalanche falls upon the column. Fight bravely, desperately as they might, there is no escape. Within a couple of hours not a man is left alive, and all the treasures of the Ebro towns have disappeared, carried off into nameless mountain hideouts. Charlemagne never avenged this catastrophe nor the death of his captain; like the Spartans at Thermopylae, like Custer's last stand, it passed into legend.

In the eleventh century, when the word crusade was coined and military expeditions against the Saracens were planned and undertaken, the epic poem 'Chanson de Roland' appeared. It told the tale of the massacre in Roncesvalles, but instead of chronicling a king's grossly incompetent misjudgment and vengeance by fellow-Christians, it extolled the knights of Christendom campaigning brilliantly against the heathen Paynim, and lamented a deceitful plot in which Roland's jealous step-father, Count Ganelon, contrives with the Saracen king to have Roland ambushed and killed. It is the savage, barbaric Paynim the reader is called on to hate; although Roland with his friend Oliver and the others of the twelve peers, fight valiantly and slaughter unimaginable numbers of the enemy, although Roland's sword Durendal accounts for most of them, and although Roland breaks all his blood-vessels blowing his horn Oliphant to summon, much too late, Charlemagne and the army back from the Gascon plains – the Paynim prevails and Roland dies. Charlemagne's fictional vengeance, of course, is frightful.

The true story is told by Charlemagne's biographer, Einhard, who uses the word Wascones to describe the Basques, possibly the first literary reference to them.

Less than a hundred years after the dispatch of Charlemagne's rearguard at Roncesvalles, the pass began to be used for a very different purpose. In a village called Compostela in a very remote district of north-western Spain, and by a miracle, the bones of St James were discovered. A shrine was built to protect them and from that time on, throughout the Middle Ages, an annual procession of pilgrims from all over Christian Europe made their hazardous way to pay their respects there. One of the routes lay over the pass of Roncesvalles, and that is the origin of the chapel and monastery at Burguete, with a community of canons to administer this staging-post for pilgrims. There is a museum attached to the canonry, which holds an important relic in Navarrese history.

King Sancho the Strong united his armies of Navarre with those of Castile and Aragon for a campaign against the Caliph Almohades: at the battle of Las Navas de Tolosa, in 1212, the Moorish chief's army was scattered, his power broken.

Almohades' tent was secured by guards bound together with stout chains; in the rout they were seized and the chains were smashed by the Navarrese Basques, becoming Sancho's trophy, and a symbol which appears on the arms and flag of Navarre to this day. The relic in the Roncesvalles museum is a fragment of these chains.

The melancholy eeriness of the mountains here may well have affected the pilgrims, on their way to Santiago de Compostela, as it no doubt chilled the hapless rearguard under Count Roland. It eventually had a similar effect on both French and British troops in the fighting that took place among these western passes in 1813.

The Duke of Wellington had so thoroughly beaten the French Army in Spain at Vitoria, capital of the Basque province of Alava, on 21 June 1813, that they had fled in complete disorder, leaving not only all their baggage, including hoards of loot, but also all their artillery. As the survivors straggled along the road home, King Joseph Bonaparte's reign came to an end. A garrison managed to hold on to Pamplona, another clung to San Sebastian, and Napoleon sent Marshal Soult to reorganize the army and defend the frontiers of France.

Wellington disposed his troops, British, Spanish and Portuguese, along the Bidassoa and Baztan, and invested the two cities. Detachments were posted in the hills, from the pass of Maya to les Aldudes and Roncesvalles. On 25 July Soult made his attempt to relieve Pamplona, advancing to the Maya and Roncesvalles passes and engaging the British troops there. At the Maya, Sir Rowland Hill and his men held out stoutly, and at Roncesvalles Byng's brigade also kept the French in check. Wellington was at Lesaca, on the Bidassoa near Vera, trying to guess at Soult's movements. He rode to the Baztan, encountering Hill's army at Irurita, down-river from Elizondo: Hill had retired from the Maya to cover Elizondo, but the French had neglected to follow him up. Wellington rode on (in the early hours of the morning; he had met Hill at 4 am) to Almandoz, just below the northern side of the Puerto de Velate, on the road to Pamplona.

There he received a message from Cole, commander of the force at Roncesvalles. He had held the position but his men were unhappy, and he was retreating to Pamplona. In his biography of Harry Smith, *Remember you are an Englishman*, Joseph Lehmann wrote that 'it was in the Pyrenees that the soldiers' nerves were strained to the breaking point. There were more desertions at this time than at any other during the long war. It was not the enemy nor the privations but the eeriness of the forbidding mountains enshrouded in mists, and the dark, isolated valleys far below, which threatened. Men accustomed to the plains or town life became fearful. At night they lost their way, or fell from narrow, winding trails into utter blackness. One ordinarily steady soldier of the 85th told Lieut. Gleig that he could face any living thing, but this haunted land was more than he could endure.'

Harry Smith, of the 95th Foot in the famous Light Division, was a remarkable young man who married a fourteen-year-old Spanish girl called Juana Maria de Los Dolores de Leon, initially to rescue her from the appalling depredations committed by the soldiers after the costly capture of Badajoz. 'In hunting, he sought the swiftest horse; in battle, he wanted to be the first to engage the enemy; in love, he wooed and married in two days.' Juana campaigned with Harry throughout the Peninsular War, and remained the most devoted of wives all their long life together. She is commemorated in the town of Ladysmith in South Africa.

The French, in this nervous action in the haunted mountains, were in a condition similar to the British, having lost themselves in the mountains, and Wellington rode on, over the Puerto de Velate, to Sorauren, a little further up the Ulzama valley from the camping-site at Oricain. Here he met Cole and the commander of the 5th Division, Picton, and here on the 28th Soult's forces, at last reunited, launched a counter-attack. His men seldom lost their nerve when Wellington was present; the line held, the French broke and were chased back to the mountains, this time north-westwards, down the Bidassoa and over the little pass of Echalar back into France. Wellington went on that summer to take both Pamplona and San Sebastian, and to cross the border into France.

A Pyrenean anomaly exists on the far side of the col. Down the long winding road to the village of **Arnéguy** it is thirteen miles, and all of them are in Spain. Generally the frontier follows the watershed but here there is a Spanish enclave on the northern side of the mountains. The border here follows the course of the Petite Nive: Valcarlos is on its left bank, so is in Spain, across the stream on the right bank is Ondaroles, so it is in France. But the frontier crosses the river just short of Arnéguy, which is therefore in France. The people of Ondaroles, being French, ought to go to Arnéguy to church, not having one themselves. They don't, they go across the river and the frontier into Valcarlos, in Spain. It is much nearer, and anyway they are all Basques, aren't they?

Once past Arnéguy and a mile or two down the widening valley following the Nive, the countryside took on a lusher, more fertile, quality, the farmhouses and cottages looked neater and brighter. **St-Jean-Pied-de-Port** (foot-of-the-pass) was a short drive away.

St-Jean's walls were of dark reddish stone; so were the inner walls, the bridges, the church and anything else built of stone. The outer walls date from the fifteenth century but in the late seventeenth there came the great Vauban, who declared them inadequate and decreed an inner ring, and a citadel on the hilltop: a town sitting astride the road up to Roncesvalles and Spain, and on the river Nive, needed to be properly defended.

St-Jean-Pied-de-Port developed during the Middle Ages: it was not the Romans' depot at the foot of the pass. This, as Belloc says, 'stood on the spot now called St-Jean-le-Vieux, two and a half miles up the lateral valley. This was the halting place of Charlemagne in the famous story...' On the western side of the village, the grassy outline of an earthen wall and the foundations of the Roman town can still be seen. St-Jean-Pied-de-Port began to develop with the pilgrim traffic.

Within the inner walls is a cobbled street called rue

St-Jacques, lined on both sides of its steep descent to the river by wonderful old Basque-style houses. It leads down to a gate through the base of the church tower, across an ancient bridge and up a street the other side of the Nive called rue d'Espagne. St-Jacques is St James, and this was the way the pilgrims went to worship at his shrine in faraway Compostela, up and over the col and down to Pamplona. Near the top of rue St-Jacques stands a gaunt stone building called the **Bishops' Prison**.

Pilgrimages during the Middle Ages became big business; the well-trodden routes were internationally recognized and surprisingly well-organized. The main routes from France into Spain, by way of Hendaye across the Bidassoa, by Roncesvalles and by Somport, were scarcely five miles at a stretch without a chapel, an oratory or a church for the pilgrims' spiritual needs, and their bodily comforts were hardly less well catered for with a series of hostels ('hospices'), inns and lodging-houses. There developed, in time, on the routes to Compostela, a kind of international tourist agency, with its own chain of hotels, health service, printed guide and highway guards, all free of charge. This prison was part of the service.

The pilgrims to Compostela, known as 'Jacquets', were not all entirely genuine. Among their number were some parasitic characters whose delight it was to take advantage of the honest piety and gullibility of their fellow-travellers. Their ploy was that of the con-man: a few acts of charity, the diffident admission of personal prosperity, the careful establishment of a totally false image of a solid, respectable, pious citizen who could be relied on for integrity, to whom you might entrust your valuables or your life. If you were unlucky, the con-men would get away with their robbery, sometimes with violence. If you became suspicious the highway guards might be at hand; you could turn the villains over to them and the false pilgrims would be flung into such a ghastly dungeon as this in St-Jean-Pied-de-Port, and serve them right.

On one visit to it I found the prison door open and pushed inside to a small, dark vestibule, with a wooden staircase leading to a closed door. There were glass cases full of military curios, swords and spears, a stuffed and mounted boar's head, and a Navarrese coat-of-arms made of real chains, to commemorate the victory at Las Navas de Tolosa. While I was looking at these relics, and glancing nervously at the unyieldingly hostile expression in the boar's face, the caretaker came in from the street with a baguette or two under her arm. She started at finding an unexpected visitor, said '*Oh, la la*', then pulled herself together, charged me the entrance fee, gave me a ticket, opened the door and switched on the taped commentary. The doorway gave on to a flight of greasy, worn stone steps (chasmally dark despite an occasional electric light), down which I stepped gingerly to a dank and dismal dungeon, lit only by a single tiny window, high up. Chains hung from the walls, the floor was of beaten earth; at the far end was a slope where prisoners could stretch out and perhaps get some sleep.

Back outside at the top of rue St-Jacques the pathway leads up to the citadel and a fine prospect of the plain, stretching away northwards into the distance. The church at the bottom of the street, whose tower straddles the pilgrims' route before it crosses the Nive, is **Notre-Dame du Pont**. It looks all of a piece, in the prevalent red stone, but although the arch-pierced tower is eleventh-century, the majority of the fabric dates from the eighteenth. It is very dark and, for a Catholic church, simple in ornament, with just the Stations of the Cross, written in Basque, on the walls; hymn-books are also in Basque. A large wooden gallery overhangs the tower end, facing the altar.

We walked along the riverside, upstream, to find the 'Pont Romane'. A dog accompanied us all the way to the little single-arched bridge and all the way back, doubtless enjoying the scenery as much as we did. 'Romane' does not mean Roman, and the bridge is not of Roman construction: it means 'romanesque', of the romantic style that was the fashion in the eleventh and twelfth centuries, which is the origin of this little bridge.

On the far side of the river we noticed the *pelota fronton*. The last rounds of the *pelota* championships are played here during July and August, and during the same period they generally put on a 'Son et Lumière' performance, using the old town's mediaeval character as a fine back-drop for its history.

St-Jean-Pied-de-Port, however tarted up for the tourist industry and full of souvenir-shops, is a useful centre for all kinds of tours by car, bicycle, or shanks' mare, either into the mountains or anywhere in the delightful Bas-Navarrese countryside.

Soule, the smallest of the Basque provinces, based on the Saison valley, was our next objective, and Mauléon, its capital, is reached by crossing a low pass called Col d'Osquich. Take the eastward road from St-Jean-Pied-de-Port; villages come in bundles in this highly fertile plain: Lacarre, Mongelos, Gamarthe, Larceveau; and between them the little hills are dotted with white farmhouses, all bright with rust-red or green shutters. The verdant meadows, greener than Ireland, bear thousands of sheep. At Larceveau the road to Mauléon, D918, turns sharp right, and it is an easy drive through Cibits, Bunus and St-Just and up the winding climb to the little Col d'Osquich; it is not such an easy walk, as I have discovered twice. From the col a beautiful pastoral scene to the north is laid out around the village of Pagolle, then the road winds down through Musculdy and Ordiarp to the flat Saison valley and Garindein, Mauléon's riverside suburb.

Soule is the least Basque in appearance of the three French provinces. The houses in Mauléon-Soule (to give its proper name), and in most of the Saison valley, have tall slate roofs, much more steeply pitched and without the deep eaves that characterize the rest of the Basque country. An odd feature of Souletin churches is that several have three-pointed bell-towers, called *trinitaires*, like the one at Gotein, farther up the valley towards Tardets.

There is a large square in the middle of Mauléon-Soule, with a war memorial at one end and the *fronton* at the other, and on one side a magnificent stone house, twin-towered, with huge steeply sloping roofs, called Hôtel d'Andurein.

It dates from the early seventeenth century. Hotel, in this connection, does not mean a house with rooms to let to passing travellers, but a large private house.

The old **castle**, called the Château-fort, sits on a crag overlooking the town and valley: this Château du Mauvais Lion is the reason why the town clusters round it: defence from marauding enemies. To reach it you must cross the swirling Saison, which here is known as the Gave de Mauléon; north of the Pyrenees, most of the shallow, rapid rivers are called *gaves*. The road divides, the main part branching off sharply right towards Tardets. To the left, beginning with a cottage called Maison des Fées, which looks like a left-over from a stage set for *Hansel and Gretel*, a metalled track climbs steeply up the side of the castle's rock. Other houses, clinging to the precipitous hillside, have bits of tower and battlement incorporated into them, and it is quite a long climb to the castle mound at the top. The feeling of height is impressive. A narrow stone bridge across a deep ditch leads to the ancient wooden door in the gatehouse: a notice instructs one to pull the venerable chain that rings, distantly, a bell. Patience is necessary, for the caretaker may not be at home, but there is a bench from which to enjoy the magnificent panorama of town and valley.

Mauléon is based on a very early form of castle, called motte-and-bailey; the motte was a high mound on which a keep was built, the bailey was longer and lower, with enough space for stables, granaries, and the garrison's living-quarters. The existing walls date from the thirteenth century and are built on the former motte; if you peer over the wall at the far end from the gatehouse you can still see the grassy shape of the bailey. In the gatehouse, which is roofed and accommodates the caretaker, there are dungeons, cells and oubliettes, no doubt suitably cold, dank and dark.

The chronicler Jean Froissart tells of his meeting one of the Lords of Mauléon, in the 1380s, known as the Bascot (Basque) de

*The castle at Mauléon-Soule*

Mauléon. He appears to have been one of those who took full advantage of the chaos in France brought by King Edward III's wars with his neighbours, in attacking and robbing friend and foe indiscriminately. 'But,' he says, 'I have always held the frontier and fought for the King of England, for my family estate lies in the Bordeaux district [Gascony: which included Soule]. Sometimes I have been so thoroughly down that I hadn't even a horse to ride, and at other times fairly rich, as luck came and went. Once Raymonnet de l'Epée and I were companion-in-arms and we held three castles near Toulouse on the frontier of Bigorre, the castle of Mauvezin, the castle of Tuzaguet and the castle of Lutilhous. They yielded us great gains for a time. Then the Duke of Anjou came and turned us out by force. Raymonnet de l'Epée was captured and went over to the French, but I remained a loyal Englishman, and shall be as long as I live.'

61

The traditional summer footgear of the Basques consists of rope-soled sandals called *espadrilles*: from the castle heights can be seen the factories that make them. The proper way of tying them should be with cross-ties round the ankle, but these days they just have a piece of blue canvas over toes and heel, like a slipper.

To visit the beauties of Ste-Engrace in the mountains, make now for **Tardets**, along the road that branches off at the foot of the castle's rock and follows the Gave upstream. Villages, Libarrenx, Gotein, Menditte, Sauguis and Trois-Villes, are not much more than a mile apart along this flat road. Houses in them are built mainly of rounded, flat stones from the Gave, laid slantwise in alternate courses, giving a herringbone pattern; roofs are slated. Trois-Villes has a château and a connection with Alexandre Dumas's *The Three Musketeers*, as will be seen in the next chapter.

According to Hilaire Belloc, 'Tardets is the market town for all the Basques of the hills, and you can never have enough of it, both of its heavenly hotel ... and for its universal shops, and for its kindly people.' For visiting tourists, it provides a quiet but delightful centre for exploring this section of the Pyrenees. We entered the square and parked in front of the arcaded terrace before a building still marked 'Hôtel des Pyrénées' in big letters, the one Belloc describes as 'one of the most delightful inns in all the mountains'. So we entered its bar, and an elderly lady seated within called the *patronne* for us; but she explained that the house was no longer an hotel. Never mind. In a corner of the square, close by a flight of steps leading down to the Gave, is the excellent Hotel Piellenia.

Although Souletin architecture is the least Basque in appearance, the Souletins themselves are regarded by the rest of the Euskadi as the most staunch of the Basques, used to preserving and practising more of their traditional songs, dances and plays than any other of the provinces. The dances are in essence similar to English Morris dances, involving set characters dressed in particular costumes, and the plays are ritual rather than natural, their subjects mainly biblical, historical or legendary, and chivalrous. The actors chant their lines amid much chorus and dance. Folk-songs are the most expressive form of Basque art. The first published work in Euskara was Bernard d'Etchepare's 'Poésies Basques', in 1545.

Stop for a drink at Café Trinquet, next to the indoor *paleta* court, a simple bar with sawdust on the floor and a few fellows in for a drink and a game of bar-football, a long way from the tourist-conscious establishments nearer the coast.

Dinner in Hotel Piellenia was delightful. After an apéritif in the bar along with the locals, it was served in the kitchen-like rear room, alongside a huge fireplace, mantelpiece gleaming with an array of brass, guns hanging on the walls, and Linge-Basque table-linen. Each course was excellent; the cheese was *brébis*, ewe's cheese, with a gentle but succulent flavour, and the wine was called 'Haitza', which in Basque means oak: a strong, dark red.

# 3

# *Aramits to Jaca*

The mountains become higher now, we are on the northern side, and there are only two more feasible passes before the High Pyrenees. On the French side the twin towns of Oloron-Ste-Marie invite a visit; on the Spanish, there is the delightful little town, Jaca. The last of the easy passes, Somport, can be used to get from Oloron to Jaca. To make any progress eastward at all from Jaca and yet keep in touch with the mountains, it is necessary to cross back into France by the much more difficult Pourtalet.

First, however, there is a double pleasure in store: drive from Tardets farther up the Saison valley, through Laguinge and Licq, to the split where two streams meet. One, the Gave de Larrau, comes in from the mountain village of Larrau to the west. If you continue past Larrau you can, with difficulty, negotiate two hazardous passes, Col d'Erroymendi and Port de Larrau, and cross into Spain, but only in high summer and with caution. It is less strenuous and more pleasurable to follow the eastern stream, the Uhaitxa, into a narrow, steep-sided valley, with huge soaring, snow-capped peaks all around. The first of the attractions to this valley lies off to the right of the road and requires walking: a parking space has been gouged out of the rock by the roadside. Near a newly built bar-restaurant standing by a dammed pool that looks like a reservoir of crème-de-menthe, a path leads into the

Gorges de Cacouette, which Belloc describes as 'one of the wonders of the Pyrenees, a cut through the limestone such as you might make with a knife into clay or cheese, with immense steep precipices on either side'. Unfortunately for us, a notice on the path's gate forbade us entry, the path had become too dangerous. It will no doubt have been repaired by summer-time, but if not there is a path farther on which takes the visitor to the upper brink of the gorge, so that he can look down into the dizzy depths and perhaps see the waterfall plummeting into them.

Having been denied the first pleasure, we determined on the second, the romanesque church of Ste-Engrace, at the very end of the valley. Below us, the waters of the Uhaitxa rushed through narrow gaps in the sheer rocks into the bottle-green pool; around us, birds sang, butterflies flitted among the spring wayside flowers, the sun shone, the sound of running water was everywhere, the peace almost tangible. Ahead of us the peak of the great Otxogorrigagne gleamed white in the sun.

As the road twisted round the side of the mountain where it dipped sharply into the ravine, we could see two prodigious clefts in the rock-mass to our right: first, where the Cacouette gorges split through, second, another slice into the mountain wall called Gorges d'Ujarre. Climbing steadily, we came eventually to Ste-Engrace. Washing was out on the lines, chickens scratched about in the yards, an occasional cat watched us pass, here and there a dog barked, but there was no sign of people. It was as if everyone had been spirited away. There was no sign of the church either until, at least a mile beyond the village, we saw it in the centre of another cluster of houses. There was a wrought-iron cross, quite large, on a terrace that overlooked the deep valley. As we stopped and inspected it, a trio of French people who had been photographing it, climbed back into their car and went on the hundred yards or so to the church.

Ste Engrace was a Spanish lady, martyred for her faith in Zaragoza in the early fourth century, when the Emperors Diocletian and Maximian were jointly ruling the Roman world.

Zaragoza, or Saragossa (which is pronounced Tharagotha anyway), is a name derived from Caesar Augusta, the town's Roman name. Although worse in the east (Diocletian's half), the persecution of Christians was widespread, extending to Gaul and Spain. Christians were given the option of making the routine sacrifice to the Roman State's gods and being issued with a certificate to prove it, or of being arrested.

In 304, the edict, previously limited to members of the clergy, was extended to all Christians, and this is when Ste Engrace met her fate. But what, one may well ask, is a Spanish saint doing in a valley on the French side of the mountains? The answer, as so often, is that we are still in the Basques' territory, and to them the mountains are no frontier: if they respected the venerated Ste Engrace on the Spanish side, they did so on the French side too.

The church dedicated to her was built a good 800 years after her martyrdom, in romanesque style: round-headed arches, barrel-vaulting overhead, cylindrical columns, capitals decorated with floral or animal designs, all cunningly intertwined and painted in coloured patterns. The term romanesque has nothing to do with Roman. It is earliest found in buildings of the tenth century, sometimes of the eleventh, and most commonly of the twelfth. The type of window used, with a round-arched head, is certainly Roman in essence, but the decoration of capitals on columns, the cylindrical nature of the columns themselves, and the typical semi-circular tympanum over doorways, carved in elaborate representations of biblical scenes, are 'romantic' rather than Roman. The French word for the style is 'romane': the French word for a romantic novel is 'un roman', so the parallel is obvious. In the little churchyard there was hardly room for the path, it was so crowded with gravestones, all in polished marble, many of them black and all inscribed with Basque family names.

There is no way out through Ste-Engrace so enjoy the walk back to the parking place, through the blissful beauty of this serene and tranquil valley. Follow the road nearly all the way back to Tardets, turning right, eastward, towards Aramits. There is

66

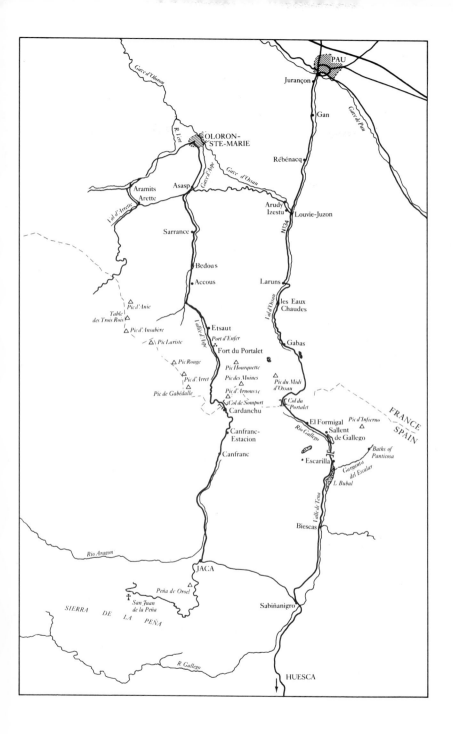

nothing dramatic or remarkable about this road; it runs through bright green, lush pastoral country in the low foothills. The first village it encounters, Montory, is in Soule, Basque country, but the next, Lanne, after an unexciting rise and fall in the landscape, is in Béarn. Aramits has largely been rebuilt now since an earthquake in 1967 in nearby Arette wrecked it. Bright against the miraculously blue sky is the great looming outline of Pic d'Anie, the first of the great mountains of the Pyrenees.

The name of **Aramits**, like that of Trois-Villes, may remind Dumas fans of one of his characters. I have heard it asserted, in Aramits, that the celebrated quartet of musketeers were real people. They weren't, but they were based on real people.

In his preface to *The Three Musketeers*, Dumas admits he based his story on an early eighteenth-century publication entitled *Memoires de Monsieur d'Artagnan*. The author had been a captain of the King's Musketeers during the reign of Louis XIII (so the memoirs were obviously published posthumously: nobody lives that long). Dumas says, 'D'Artagnan relates, that on his first visit to M. de Tréville, Captain of the Royal Musketeers, he met three young men in the ante-chamber, serving in the illustrious corps into which he solicited the honour of being admitted, and bearing the names of Athos, Porthos, and Aramis.' Dumas had also used another book of recollections of the period, *Memoires de M. le Comte de la Fère* and in its pages he found the names of all three musketeers, the Comte de la Fère being Athos himself.

Dumas used the names, but altered history to make a better story. In his book, the events, from the Duke of Buckingham's flirtation with Queen Anne to the siege of la Rochelle and his assassination, run continuously; in fact, three years separated the two. There is no evidence, furthermore, of the bold musketeers' part in either occurrence. According to Dumas, 'D'Artagnan ... made every effort to find out who Athos, Porthos, and Aramis really were, for under one of those assumed appellations, each of these young men concealed his real name.'

D'Artagnan was a Gascon, as was 'M. de Troisvilles, as

his family was yet called in Gascony'. In fact, the other three were too.

Béarn in the early seventeenth century was a small place with a growing population but a poor economy and, like all such places, found a readily exportable commodity in young men. Gascons had for centuries sold their services as mercenaries, and several young Béarnais of good family, which is to say either traditional landowners or rich merchants who had bought themselves into landowning society, went to Paris and took arms for the king. One of these was Isaac de Portau of Pau (Porthos), another was Armand de Sillègue d'Autevielle (Athos: Autevielle is near Sauveterre), and a third, Henri, was the lay abbé of Aramits (Aramis). Captain de Tréville was in fact lord of the manor of Trois-Villes, the village near Tardets. So the four musketeers did exist, but the four who helped to preserve the good name of Anne d'Autriche were the inventions of Alexandre Dumas.

The road from Aramits is wide and fast, crossing from time to time the River Vert on its way to join the Gave d'Oloron, and heading for the twin town of **Oloron – Ste-Marie**, with its splendid cathedrals.

Oloron – Ste-Marie is now administered as one town, but until 1858 the two communities, on either side of the Gave d'Oloron, existed independently. The story is a little complicated.

Two rivers, the Gaves d'Aspe and d'Ossau, meet a little below the town to form the Gave d'Oloron. The hilly tongue of land there provided a good defensible position and was in all probability a settlement of the Elloronians, one of the Nine Peoples, when the Romans began their conquest of Gaul. In 56 BC Publius Crassus, one of Caesar's lieutenants, with the 7th Legion, invaded Aquitania, and legend has it that he made camp on this site, establishing it as the regional capital, Illuro. As the Romans extended their dominion over Spain, and as Illuro commanded the road to the Somport pass, which they called Summus Portus or Summus Pyrenaeus, to Zaragoza, its strategic importance caused it to flourish. When the Roman Empire became officially Christian in 395, the first of the local bishoprics was established here. Illuro was distinguished by being the seat of one Gratus, subsequently canonized.

Illuro survived the waves of Vandals, Visigoths and Franks who overran Gaul and Spain and destroyed the administration of the Western Empire. Partly Christian themselves, albeit heretically, they did not upset the established Church, but a few hundred years later Illuro was an obvious target for the Moorish Saracens, who came the other way, over Somport, and sacked the town. A hundred years after that, in 843, the terrible Norsemen came up the rivers Garonne and Adour and the Gaves, looting and destroying, and Illuro ceased to exist. But because life went on and because the crossing-place of the Gaves by the Somport road still brought business, the new town, Ste-Marie, began to grow up on the west bank of the Gave d'Aspe. Later, in the eleventh century, a viscount of Béarn, Centulle V, refounded the old town on the east bank as Oloron.

The viscounty of Béarn had developed from two very small areas: the valley of the Gave de Pau near Lescar, which used to be Beneharnum and also had a Roman bishop, and the country around Morlaas, called Vic-Bilh. In Nine Peoples' times, the inhabitants were known as Civitas Benarnensium. In the ninth century, when the Norsemen were bringing terror into the fair land of France, there developed a system of protection in return for land known as feudality, the name had become Béarn and the protector was a viscount. Centulle V created the 'For d'Oloron' in 1080, the oldest municipal charter in France, founded the church of Ste-Croix, installed a bishop in it again, and took over control of the three Pyrenean valleys south of the town. Within this framework and under the rule of successive viscounts, the two towns prospered.

The **Cathedral of Ste-Marie** was completed in 1102, which explains why it still has a magnificent romanesque porch; but it was burnt in the early thirteenth century, struck by lightning in the fourteenth, enlarged in 1602 and restored in 1880. The finest feature is still the porch, survivor of the original foundation by Viscount Gaston IV, on his return from the First Crusade. Beneath an elaborately decorated, round-headed arch, the doorway is divided by a supporting column with carved caryatids representing chained Saracens, depicted as though they are forever holding up the entire cathedral. Above them is a great tympanum representing the Descent from the Cross. On the two semi-circular outer rims of the main arch, in minute detail, are figurines showing the vision of St John; the 24 Elders are playing assorted musical instruments, then other figures from the Apocalypse. Surmounting columns to right and left of the porch are a mounted knight of unrecognizable features (through erosion or vandalism or both) but who is probably Gaston IV himself, and a monster of some fearful type who is swallowing a man head-first. All this wonderful sculpture is in Pyrenean marble. Inside, the cathedral is dark, but there are more sculptures showing the miracles of the Elloronian bishop, St Gratus, and there is a wealth of decorative painting, on the walls, on the apse, even on the ceiling. Banks of candles were burning before the altars.

From Ste-Marie walk down Rue de Révol to the bridge over the Gave d'Aspe into Oloron. From the bridge pause to enjoy the view of the serrated outline of the great peaks surrounding the Vallée d'Aspe – Pic d'Anie, Pic du Midi d'Ossau over on the left, and all the other giants in between – rearing silvery heads in the bright sunlight, a vividly dramatic backdrop to the old town.

Oloron's steep rue Labarraque, lined with ancient stone houses on either side, is named after the famous chemist, Antoine Germain Labarraque. A plaque on his birthplace, No 46, commemorates him. At the top of the road is Place St-Pierre, a favourite spot for the town elders to play *boules*. The former church of St-Pierre is now a garage selling cars. The square is below the crown of Oloron's hill, where stands the **Cathedral of Ste-Croix**, which although frequently patched up in the course of its 900-year existence, is basically the same building that

Centulle V began in 1080. The guide-book of the Syndicat d'Initiative says that 'the visitor will remark the unity of style, the harmonious proportions of this romanesque edifice, and the severity, the nobility of its lines, which will impose on his memory'. Another way of saying that it is rather plain, lacking the inspired artistic flamboyance of its sister across the river. When we peered in its doorway, the whole of the interior was being uprooted, sand everywhere, planks along which workmen were wheeling barrows, and huge flagstones leaning against the walls. Entry was understandably prohibited. Outside in the warm air there was a little green, a bench and that magnificent panorama of great mountains. Away down the hill to the left is an ancient tower called Tour de Grède, all that is left of the former bishops' palace.

Summus Portus was the only pass in this region until that of le Perthus, to the east, which Hannibal used. In the Middle Ages it became important again for the passage of pilgrims to Santiago de Compostela, and in 1108 Gaston IV built a lodging place for them, called Hospital of Santa Cristina, on the Spanish side of the pass; its remains are still visible. Canfranc, on the Spanish side of Somport, was the centre for the bulk of pilgrim traffic over the mountains until the easier routes at the eastern end became safe from the depredations of Basque brigands.

To reach Somport you must take the road to Vallée d'Aspe, following on one side the shallow, rushing river, on the other, the old Canfranc railway, opened in 1928, with a five-mile tunnel under the pass. The line was re-opened in 1950, after the Second World War, but it looks far from prosperous today: the lines are rusty and the track grown over.

The Vallée d'Aspe, although bigger than most Pyrenean valleys on the northern, French side, bears the same characteristics as all, sharply divided by very narrow gorges into two or more level basins. In the smaller valleys and on the higher levels where there is pasture for livestock and no houses, they are called *jasses*. The larger and lower ones, like this bearing the villages of Asasp, Sarrance, Bedous and Accous, are called *plains* or *plans*, consisting of a level floor more or less wide, bordered by steep mountains on either side, and ending in a rocky gate through which the valley stream gushes in a torrential cascade. The whole physical configuration suggests that in remote times these *plans* were lakes, filled by the waters of the rivers in stages, as they thrust from the mountains down to the plains. The Vallée d'Aspe is fertile and supports many villages. Beyond Bedous and Accous, tucked into the low foothills, the valley narrows and the level rises squeezing road, railway and river together. At Etsaut the valley becomes a deep gorge; on the east side of it, perched high on the craggy, vertiginously sheer rocks, is a castle, Fort du Portalet. The gorge itself is called Port d'Enfer, and hellish indeed would have been the lot of the unfortunate soldiers on garrison duty in that inaccessible, lonely, frightening and terrible outpost. The last village is Urdos, where the French customs wave you through, and you start to climb, slowly at first, then in the familiar zig-zag, gaining height, crawling up among the savage, broken-toothed, menacing mountains, Pic Hourquette, Pic des Moines, Pic d'Arnousse and Pic de Gabedalle, all well over 7,000 feet. At the top is a Spanish frontier post. The descent on the Spanish side is much less strenuous after the first, sharp hairpin bend, and you come at once to Candanchu, a winter-sports centre. The popularity of skiing in the Pyrenees has increased greatly in the past few years, to the profit of those engaged in its service, but to the detriment of the landscape in certain places; hotels and apartment blocks are sprouting everywhere, like mushrooms in the night.

The road winds down to Canfranc-Estacion, where the railway emerges from its tunnel, and on to Canfranc itself, at the head of the Aragon river, the river that gave its name to one of the strongest of the mediaeval kingdoms of Spain, which led the rest to the reconquest of Spain from the Moors and the eventual union of the country under one king. The road and the little, forlorn railway follow the bubbling waters down a wild valley and into a brown-tinged plain by easy, long stretches to Jaca. To the south of Jaca looms a great mass of hill called Peña de Oroel, part of the Sierra de la Peña that turns the Aragon westward to the plain of the Ebro.

**Jaca** is one of only three sizeable towns in the Spanish Pyrenees. In the east the River Segre performs the same kind of journey as the Aragon, running westward along the Sierra del Cadi, and first there is Puigcerda close to the French frontier and the high Puymorens pass, then Seo de Urgel, close to the Andorran valleys, both of them in the plain of Cerdanya. Jaca commands the southern approaches to Somport and the western passage along the Aragon valley called the Canal de Berdun. This important situation guaranteed it municipal status in the Roman world and its name, Iacca, by the second century.

In 1033 King Ramiro I of Aragon chose it to be his capital and began to build its **cathedral**, the first major romanesque church in Spain.

The interior of the cathedral is sombre but magnificent, with great Corinthian columns, high, small windows and many chapels. One of them, the Chapel of San Miguel, has intricate alabaster figures sculpted in 1523 by the Florentine, Giovanni Moreto. The main altar-piece is a sculpture by Juan de Ancheta, of 1575, said to show the influence of Michelangelo's Moses. Very little of the Italian Renaissance penetrated into the Spanish Pyrenees, largely because on the French side it was impeded by a strong Protestant movement. The cathedral cloister, which still shows traces of its twelfth-century construction, is covered in. This rare indication of awareness of Mother Nature's sterner side by men of the Church was probably dictated by the fact that Jaca is high and has hard winters. Some of the cloister windows are even glazed, with thin alabaster.

The cathedral is approached along a short street by the side of a new Hotel Mur, which has some splendid exterior woodwork but is certainly not the 'house of Constancia Mur' known both to Belloc and J. B. Morton. Nearby are streets of old houses, some arcades and a seminary for priests. Jaca also has a Summer

University and a Centre for Pyrenean Studies, run by the University of Zaragoza; many students of all nations are said to attend. Opposite Hotel Mur is a road leading to the low-walled citadel, open to the public at certain hours, its garrison of soldiers still guarded by a sentry.

Before leaving Jaca, you should, if you have time, take an excursion to the monastery of **San Juan de la Peña**, up to the formidable Peña de Oroel, by a track which leads off left from the main road west out of town, about five and a half miles along it. There was a monastery built here in the ninth century, when the Christians were dominated by the Moorish Muslims and their form of service and style of religion were known as Mozarabic. One arch remains of this original building, the entrance to the twelfth-century cloister; the church itself is of the eleventh and twelfth centuries. As San Juan was in the forefront of the reconquest, this was the first monastery in Spain where the monks could chant the Roman rite instead of the Mozarabic. In the late seventeenth century the monks built a new, baroque structure, up on the plateau above the old monastery. During the Peninsular wars, French troops arrived hoping for plunder, but found that all the treasures, accumulated over centuries, had been taken for safety to Jaca. They burnt the monastery, which has in modern times been rebuilt as a State Parador by the province of Huesca. Below the monastery is Santa Cruz de la Seros, which derives its name from the nuns, *las Sorores*, for whom it was founded in 984 by King Sancho Garces of Aragon. The church was built later, in 1076, but the sisters moved to Jaca during the sixteenth century.

To regain France by the Col du Pourtalet, take the road east from Jaca, and before you reach the little industrial town of Sabiñanigo, turn left, following the Gallego river northward up the Valle de Tena towards the mountains. You pass through the market-town of Biescas, then by a lake (a dammed part of the river) on your right, called Bubal. At the village of Escarilla, turn right.

The road from Escarilla is steep and twisting; it goes through a gorge called the Garganta del Escalar and emerges at the Baths of Panticosa. This is a long-established thermal resort; rain-water, heated below ground in deep faults, where it has absorbed sundry beneficial chemical substances, reaches the surface again as mineral water. The lake here is one of over a thousand in the High Pyrenees, in a ring of mountains like Argualas and Infierno, the Peak of Hell.

After Escarilla the road goes through a tunnel, emerges by another lake on the Gallego, passes by Sallent de Gallego and the Spanish customs post at El Formigal, and climbs up to the Col du Pourtalet to wind round the great southern flank of the Pic du Midi d'Ossau. This is some of the wildest country in all the Pyrenees and is now a National Park. Here is the last refuge of the Pyrenean bear, and there are wild boars, eagles, and izards or Pyrenean chamois.

Down you go now, through Gabas, down the Val d'Ossau to les Eaux Chaudes, another thermal station pioneered by one Théophile de Bordeu. This Béarnais doctor, who lived in the eighteenth century, was known as 'the Voltaire of Medicine' because he fought as vehemently as Voltaire did with words for the sake of a more scientific approach to medicine. He had great faith in the curative properties of Pyrenean mineral waters, and as he was a persuasive writer he managed to induce many of his contemporaries to take their over-loaded constitutions to be purged at the thermal stations he founded.

At the opening of the valley stands Laruns, a pleasant little town, and the N134, the road to Pau.

# 4

# *Pau*

The old provinces of France were destroyed by the Revolution, to be replaced by Napoleon's new *départements*. This western end of the Pyrenees is called *Pyrénées Atlantiques,* but old traditions die hard: while the Basques insist on their three *Pays Basque* provinces, the people to their east prefer their ancient designation, *Béarnais.* Their capital is Pau, the biggest town in Béarn and the best centre for touring it.

A few miles downstream from Laruns, on the Vallée d'Ossau road, you could take D918 at Louvie-Juzon, forking left, and enjoy a visit to the extensive forest called Bois du Bager, accompanying the Gave d'Ossau on its way to Oloron. The road has as many twists as if it were climbing a mountain, but the woods are mainly deciduous , oak, ash and beech, instead of the otherwise ubiquitous conifers, which makes a pleasant change.

On the wide valley road towards Pau is the village of Rébénacq, on the little River Nez which the road follows all the way to the Gave de Pau. There were two bars in the square by the church, and we chose the livelier, patronized mostly by the drivers of the lorries parked outside. It was a rough, country bar; the truckers were sitting down in the little dining-room, a workman was rebuilding the stone fireplace, the ham sandwiches were succulent and the bonhomie flowed as liberally as the excellent beer. Chez Palu would probably not earn any marks from the Michelin Guide, but it was a hundred per cent good value.

A little farther on down this swift, fine highway lies Jurançon, whose vineyards are now acquiring a much wider reputation. Across the Gave and you are in the centre of Pau, Place Grammont. On the way in to town, before Jurançon, you pass through an unattractive village called Gan. There is a connection, however improbable, between Gan and Place Grammont, and it involves the famous Henri IV, King of France.

A fifteenth-century count of Béarn, Gaston IV, ambitious for dominion and status, married Eleanor, a princess of Navarre. Their son, François-Fébus, was crowned King of Navarre in Pamplona in 1481. His kingdom, sitting astride the Pyrenees, was in a particularly dangerous position, since a strong France had brought all its south-western provinces except Béarn under control, and the kings of Spain had unified most of the Iberian peninsula. François-Fébus and his successors had the problem of maintaining their little kingdom's neutrality against two powerful forces, one on either side. His daughter Catherine was married to the French lord, Jean d'Albret, the Spanish king refused to accept garrisons of French troops south of the Pyrenees, so Spanish Navarre was lost to her. Her son, Henri II d'Albret (1517–55) observed that his kingdom was 'like a flea between two monkeys'. He managed nevertheless to make it an oasis of peace and prosperity in the desert of warfare between the rising powers of Spain and France, but realized that in all probability it would not last. A series of dynastic marriages with the royal house of France ensured that, if Béarn's independence were to be lost, then at least there might be a Béarnais king of France one day. Henri II himself married the sister of François I of France, Marguerite of Angoulême, in 1527; in 1548, their daughter Jeanne d'Albret married Antoine of Bourbon; their son Henri, when he succeeded to the throne of Navarre in 1572, married Marguerite of Valois, the royal family whose male line was destined to fail, making Henri its sole successor.

It was during the reign of Queen Jeanne d'Albret (1555–72) that the Protestant cause took hold in Béarn and other regions north of the Pyrenees. Jeanne formally announced her own conversion in 1560; she created an academy in Orthez, the former capital of Béarn (Gaston IV had moved it to Pau), in the manner of Calvin's at Geneva, and in 1568 obtained a majority in the Béarnais assembly for the conversion of her people. The Catholic King of France, Charles IX, reacted by invading Béarn, but his soldiers were beaten at Navarrenx in 1569.

Jeanne's version of Protestantism was narrowly Puritan and self-righteously intolerant: her son Henri, future King Henri III of Navarre and Henri IV of France, had inherited the more easy-going traditions of his grandfather Henri II. He was not at all averse to having a good time while he could, conducting more or less clandestine affairs with any young lady he fancied. One of these came from Gan, and her name was Corisande d'Andouins.

Corisande was born in a fine Renaissance house in the square, recently built by her rich father. She was attractive but in that certain way that causes a discerning man to say to himself, 'Yes, she's pretty enough now, but by the time she's thirty-five or so, she'll be plain, fat, and probably greedy too.' Corisande was not her real name. Romantic poetry was popular in the late sixteenth century, telling tales full of mediaeval chivalry and high-minded passion. Corisande was the name of one of the heroines, and its new bearer had the less than high-minded ambition of becoming the mistress of the heir to the throne. Her wealthy family's exalted connections ensured that she achieved it. Corisande won the distinction of claiming Henri's affections for longer than anyone else, even after he had married Marguerite de Valois and even after he had become King Henri III of Navarre. Not until 1587 did he finally break his association with her, before succeeding to the French throne in 1589. It was then that Corisande married the Comte de Grammont, and no doubt became plain, fat and greedy. Her son was a mayor of Bayonne, and later Grammonts were governors of the province of Béarn, as it became after 1620.

Parking is at a premium in Pau, or at least in the Place Grammont. Having decided to stay in the Hotel de Gramont (one m, reason unexplained) in a corner of the square, the pretty young receptionist said I could put the car on the outside of the pedestrian crossing, next to the stream of traffic. It seemed a bit perilous but it was just off the road and no one seemed to mind. There were two crossings, the one next to the car and another at right-angles to it, across the main road, with a novel talking crossing light: at the red light, it said, *'Arrêts, piétons'* and when the green man showed, it changed to *'Allez, piétons'*. We could hear this from our room, on the corner exactly over this phenomenon. Light sleepers might be advised to request a room at the back.

The great **Château de Pau** stands high above the swirling Gave – high above the railway station too, now – and commands one of the most striking views of the Pyrenees of any sub-Pyrenean town.

Castles of various sorts have existed on this site since the dim and unrecorded days of Béarnais history, and took some kind of traceable form in the twelfth century. The present building is an amalgam of several distinct periods. The entrance is between two towers, connected by a classical three-arched gateway. The right-hand tower, and the gateway, of stone, are little more than a century old; the left-hand tower is of brick and dates from the fourteenth century. It was built from 1370 onwards by Viscount Gaston III of Béarn. Gaston IV, who died in 1472, has already been encountered in this chapter, but as we have seen in Chapter 3, another Gaston IV had apparently built a cathedral in Ste-Marie in 1102, so an explanation is required. The situation was similar to that in Scotland and England, where James VI of Scotland became James I of England, because a James had never before been King of England. Those with long memories will at once recall that round about 1952, Scots with even longer memories placed explosive devices in their new letter-boxes because they had EIIR on them: no Elizabeth, they said, had ever been Queen of Scotland before, so the letter-boxes ought to be marked with EIR. In 1290 Viscount Gaston VII of Béarn died, leaving no male heir. One of his daughters had married Count Roger-Bernard of Foix, who now became viscount of Béarn as well, uniting the two Pyrenean provinces. Counts of Foix had never been Gaston before, and as soon as one was (the son of Roger-Bernard, in 1302), he was called Gaston I. Béarnais historians, of course, went on writing about Gaston VIII, IX and X and so on, and if they had had pillar-boxes no doubt they would have blown them up.

Gaston III of Foix-Béarn was one of history's more enlightened despots. The Hundred Years' War placed him, and his father Gaston II, in a dilemma because as counts of Foix they owed homage to the king of France but as viscounts of Béarn they owed it to the duke of Gascony, alias the king of England, at present on opposing sides in the long struggle. The Gastons solved their problem by refusing homage to the king of England, taking advantage of the French king's preoccupation with the war, and enjoying what amounted to autonomy. Gaston III, who gained the additional name of Phoebus, successfully defied the Black Prince's attempts to bring him into line simply by playing for time and waiting until the prince so weakened his army on other campaigns that he could not invade Béarn. He eventually acquired control over his neighbouring provinces of Soule and Bigorre, and administered his scattered dominions in the interests of his people, dispensing with the usual assemblies and ruling as a despot, albeit a benevolent one. We will meet him again at Foix but since his first concern was protection of his lands, defences were built, and this castle of Pau took new and stronger shape. Brick was a very unusual material in the fourteenth century, but came to be used by many later castle-builders.

King Henri II of Navarre next transformed the place in 1529. The former court of Béarn had been the castle of Orthez, a tall, bleak, mediaeval tower; but since Henri's marriage to the French princess Marguerite d'Angoulême, sister of King François I, he

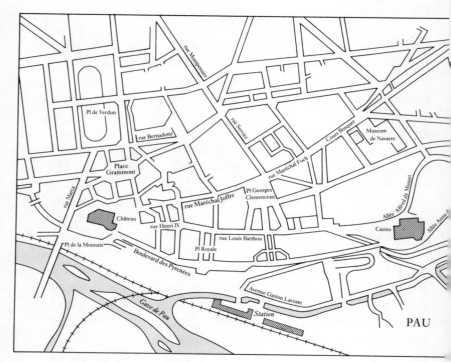

felt something more suitable to so refined a lady was called for. He had the castle of Pau altered and enlarged, terraces made where before there was a tilting-yard, huge windows on to the Pyrenean panorama put in instead of loop-holes for archers, and straight flights of stairs instead of spirals. All was accomplished in the new Renaissance style, and ceilings were plaster-moulded with the letters H and M prominently displayed. The work lasted from 1529 to 1535; it transformed a military stronghold as uncomfortable as that at Orthez into a fine, modern royal palace and transformed Pau into the Béarnais capital of his kingdom of Navarre. This 'flea between two monkeys' could benefit, at least temporarily, from the monkeys' incessant conflict, because the kingdom stood astride the Pyrenees on a clear route through from the basin of the Garonne to that of the Ebro. Henri II reorganized the Béarnais defence system, its legal system, its monetary practice and its agriculture. He encouraged farmers from other parts of France to settle in Béarn and teach its peasants that other forms of economy did exist beyond their traditional pasturage and stock-breeding: for example, the vine. Thus the vineyards of Jurançon and Monein came into being, as did other industries, such as the iron-mines of Ossau and Ouzom and the textiles of Oloron. However, although he had brought the Renaissance and prosperity to Béarn, he seldom managed to bring his wife Marguerite, so courtly Renaissance enlightenment did not penetrate much farther into the Pyrenees than Pau.

The rooms in the castle are well restored, lavishly furnished and decorated. On the ground floor there is a former guard-room called the Room of the Hundred Guests, with a vast table which can actually accommodate that number of diners. This was the room in which Louis XIII in 1620 formally declared that the Kingdom of Navarre no longer existed, that Béarn's autonomy was over and it was now a province of France. In another room, on a higher floor, his father, Henri IV, had been born, heir to the thrones of Navarre and France; there is a huge tortoise-shell in the room which, according to tradition, acted as his cradle.

After 1620 the castle was a home for the governors of Béarn but it was ruined during the Revolution. It was repaired in the nineteenth century by King Louis-Philippe, who added another tower on the western end, and further embellished by the Emperor Napoleon III, who stayed in it with his Empress Eugénie, the last crowned heads to reside here. The rooms are splendid: rich, red wall-hangings, elegant chairs upholstered in glowing colours, huge beds with glorious hangings, sculptures, paintings, ceramic vases and, above all, the tapestries.

If nothing else of all this appeals, the Castle of Pau is worth visiting just to see its collection of **tapestries**. These are mainly Gobelins but some are reproductions of earlier Flemish masterpieces, and all have the same subtlety of touch, colours glowing delicately, exquisitely, so that when you look upon them, you are at once transported out of the twentieth century into some ethereal mystic Golden Age, into the Arcadia of shepherds, satyrs, fauns and nymphs, of gods and goddesses, where 'Eternal summer gilds them yet'. Or you are in the deep green forests of the Middle Ages, where huntsmen pause from the chase in some cool glade, their dogs frolic while their ladies bring out refreshments; a minstrel plays, a distant horn sounds, a deer darts fleetingly through the foliage, a noble lord bends his lips over a fair lady's white hand. You stand before a burning, bright desert where a man in animal skins speaks to a crowd of wondering peasants: St John the Baptist, his very gestures proclaiming his urgent sincerity.

The tapestries of Pau are magic, sheer magic.

On the top floor of the castle there is a **museum**, for which one needs a separate ticket. Rather cramped for space, it contains, on a smaller scale, the kind of things pertaining to the Béarnais that you see of the Basques in the Musée Basque in Bayonne. In addition, there are stuffed fauna: a grim-visaged Pyrenean bear and an izard; birds, insects and butterflies to vary the diet of pots and pans, instruments and tools, peculiarities of dress and relics of local artists, poets and authors. One of the poets was Alfred de Vigny.

Some of the officers of Wellington's army, seeking a milder climate for their retirement, remembered Pau – its winter clemency to their arthritis, its splendid prospect of the mountains, the hunting, the propinquity of thermal stations for their health (and that of their wives), and the kindness of the people, who appreciated Wellington's insistence that his men should pay for whatever they wanted. Gradually they returned to settle, and formed a small colony. One of the first was a certain Bunbury, an ex-Indian army officer, whose daughter met and fell in love with de Vigny, garrisoned there with the French army since 1823. He does not seem to have enjoyed Pau much. 'I live,' he wrote, 'among my mountains like one of their bears.' He married Miss Bunbury in 1825. Lamartine liked the place much better. He was there for just one day in Pau in 1841 but wrote later, 'There may be seen the most beautiful landscape, as Naples is the most beautiful seascape.'

In 1842 one Dr Alexander Taylor published in London a work called 'On the curative influence of the climate of Pau'. The thermal stations prospered mightily, as delicate constitutions by the hundred were soused in the waters of Eaux-Chaudes, Eaux-Bonnes, Cambo and Argelès-Gazost. The foreigners' money was once more welcome to Pau because Béarn was going through hard times: the railway from Bayonne to Irun had been opened and it took away all the trade that for centuries had passed through Béarn to Spain and the Pyrenean passes. Between 1846 and 1900 nearly 30,000 Béarnais emigrated.

During the period after the fall of the Second Empire in 1870, when Napoleon III's paper power was torn apart by the astute and ruthless Bismarck, the British colony in Pau began again to flourish. The **Boulevard des Pyrénées** was constructed, the parade that runs along the ridge below the castle and above the Gave, displaying to full advantage the celebrated view of the mountains. The Casino was built, and the grand hotels between it and the castle. It was in this Belle Epoque, towards the end of the century, that the English and the Scots introduced the noble art of rugby football, and the Palois, fascinated, took it up themselves. Look at the home-teams of the present rugby XV of France: the majority are in the south-west and that region is still the heartland of French rugby. The colony died at the beginning of the Great War of 1914-18, when the British went home. Gruesome numbers of the Béarnais died, too, as the village war memorials testify.

After the castle tour we revived at the Café de la Coupole in Place Clemenceau, the main square. It was a typical, classy café, with a glassed-in area fronting the pavement, potted palms, liveried waiters and marble-topped round tables. It was where friends met friends, during *l'heure de l'apéritif*, where husbands met wives and other assignations were kept. Though one made conversation, sipped one's *pastis*, glanced at the newspaper and smoked one's cigarette, the real pleasure lay in watching *le monde* pass by just outside in the street.

For dinner we returned to one of the small streets near the castle, and the Restaurant O Gascon. A line of laid tables down the centre of this hostelry proclaimed that a party was expected, but we were served before they arrived by two young men who might well have been the sons of Madame la Patronne. During the second course eighteen good-looking, healthy young fellows came in. 'Must be a rugby club dinner,' we said. The bottles circulated, the conviviality began to rise in decibel-rating. We asked Madame who they were. 'Students,' she said, 'at a local college where they learn to play rugby.'

Cheerful good living has a long tradition in Béarn. Despite centuries of penury, in the rare intermission periods, such as the reign of Henri II, the Béarnais liked to live well, to enjoy good food, good wine, good sport and perhaps a little light philandering on the way. No doubt this is one of the reasons why the Béarnais like to remember Henri IV whom they call, in their dialect, 'Noustre Henric'.

Henri had the misfortune to inherit the throne of France at a time when his countrymen were tearing one another apart in the interests of the Christian faith. Henri's mother, Queen Jeanne d'Albret of Navarre, was typical of the narrow and intolerant minds thrown up during this wretched era: her victory in 1569 led her to issue *Ordonnances écclésiastiques* in 1571, confiscating all Church property, imposing Calvanistic practices on the whole of Béarn, and totally banning Catholicism. The majority of the Béarnais supported her; acknowledging that some of her Navarrese subjects were Basques, she caused the writer Leiçarraga to translate the New Testament into Basque, and had it printed in La Rochelle, the Huguenot stronghold.

During the summer of 1572 Queen Jeanne and her son Henri were in Paris with the object of marriage between Henri and the king's sister, Marguerite of Valois. On the eve of St Bartholomew's Day (24 August) thousands of Huguenots (Protestants) were massacred in the Paris streets: the ailing

Jeanne d'Albret died, and the new King Henri III of Navarre, as a Protestant, was imprisoned. Charles IX of France issued an edict returning Navarre to the Catholic faith, and ordered the lord of Grammont to expel all Calvinistic pastors. However, the Béarnais managed again to frustrate the French king's will by beating Grammont's forces. Henri's sister, Catherine of Bourbon, acted as regent in Béarn until he was released: as sister of the French king, Henri's new bride Marguerite of Valois was of course a Catholic, and obviously there would be severe sectarian problems between her and her Protestant husband. When the couple eventually took up residence in the Castle of Pau, Marguerite asked for some Catholic Béarnais to assist in a private mass held for her there. So deeply entrenched was Protestant zeal in Pau that even she could not prevent them from being arrested. Disgusted with the 'little Geneva', as she called it, she left Pau and swore never to return.

But how could this fierce religious independence last, when political and economic independence was rapidly vanishing? Navarre's king was married to a French princess; craftsmen and artisans had been introduced from France to stimulate new crafts and industries; it was to France that thousands of Béarnais emigrated to make their fortunes, often by fighting for the Catholic king of France.

In 1589 that Catholic king, Henri III (1574–89), last male heir of the House of Valois, was murdered. The only possible successor, thanks to the dynastic marriages of the royal House of Navarre, was Henri III of Navarre, who now became Henri IV of France as well (again, similarly to James VI of Scotland becoming James I of England too). As a Protestant, however, Henri could not even enter Paris, let alone be crowned king. In 1593 he took the only possible course, of abjuring his Protestantism. 'Paris,' he is said to have observed, 'is worth a mass.' He promised the Pope to return his native land, Béarn, to Rome, and in 1599 his mother Queen Jeanne's laws were overturned. But Henri had the good sense to keep the Béarnais on his side by giving them back their autonomy, for his lifetime at least; he decided that Béarn and Bas-Navarre should be 'disjointed and separate from our House of France'. Henri was also at pains to ensure that although he had become an obedient son of the Church, his former co-religionists should not be made to suffer. His Edict of Nantes of 1598 had guaranteed the safety of Huguenots by granting them liberty of conscience and equality before the law, and ensured that they got it by insisting that courts of justice should contain elements of both factions.

Henri, as we have seen, was not exactly suitable Calvinist material. He had never liked his wife much and when he had tired of Corisande d'Andouins, he transferred his affections for a while to another mistress, Gabrielle d'Estrées. His popularity, especially among his fellow Béarnais, derived partly from this cheerful disregard for the proprieties and his equal scorn of danger. To the ordinary people he was everything they admired in a king: good-humoured, good-living, accessible (as far as possible) and slightly vulgar. His heart was in the right place: he wished that every peasant should have 'a chicken in the pot of a Sunday'. To most of the undernourished and downtrodden peasantry of France this was no more than a dream, and remained so. Perhaps if Henri had lived in less acrimonious times he could have made it possible, and laid the foundations for a very different kind of society, one that would not have been so intransigent that only violent and bloody revolution could alter it. Unhappily, however, he was surrounded by bigots, fanatics and pretenders to either religious persuasion who were actually only self-seekers, and he had to steer a precarious course between them, avoiding would-be assassins. One of them, Ravaillac, murdered him in 1610.

In the room in the Castle of Pau where he was born there are several busts and portraits of 'Noustre Henric'. They show a man high of forehead and firm of chin, with slightly tilting eyebrows and a humorous, quizzical expression, with a trace of cynicism. Compare him with his grandson, Charles II of England: Charles certainly had all of Henri's love of a good life (and even more mistresses) but lacked his determined statecraft, still more any genuine concern for his less fortunate subjects. Charles was clever, but his reputation as a cynical libertine cannot be salvaged.

Largely thanks to the attentions both of the British colony and of the Emperor Napoleon III, Pau has retained its pre-eminence: once capital of Béarn, it is now capital of *Pyrénées-Atlantiques*. Its administrative importance has been extended within the last 35 years since the discovery of copious reserves of natural gas at Lacq, twelve miles downriver on the Gave de Pau. It is also a natural centre for tourism: the warm, gentle climate that attracted the British colonists in the last century still prevails, its situation, commanding the roads towards the Pyrenees facilitates day-excursions, and its stately hotels and elegant streets make it pleasant to stay in. Not for nothing did Napoleon III create the Boulevard des Pyrénées, running along the front of the castle, above the river: from it you may see the mountains ranging from end to end of the southern horizon, showing such a range of colours and shades, especially at dawn and sunset, that many visitors, if not content with photography, have rushed off to fetch their paints and canvases.

Before photography there was no alternative to the paint-box, and the Musée des Beaux-Arts, at the far end of Rue Maréchal Joffre, on the corner of Parc Beaumont, exhibits some of the results. Entry to the splendid, monumental building is free. You climb the steps in front, passing between two sculpted cows, into the elegant foyer. The majority of the paintings are by nineteenth- and twentieth-century artists, but there is also a room-full of Rubens sketches, including one for 'The Fall of the Damned' and Achilles killing Hector, among sundry other mythological subjects. There are some Guillaumins, a Degas of a gentleman testing the quality of cotton in New Orleans, a Picasso pen-sketch, and a Matisse pencil-sketch of a nude Aurora. The two latter artists have a strong Pyrenean connection, as we shall see later. There are also several local Pyrenean scenes by one

Victor Galos (1828–79), a native of Pau. Rooms upstairs are occupied by abstract and modern works which may not be to everyone's taste.

Another notable Palois is commemorated in the house where he was born, in a street named after him, not far from Place Grammont. This is Jean Bernadotte.

The number of Béarnais who, like the seventeenth-century musketeers, found fame and fortune outside the province probably exceeds those who stayed there. Jean-Baptiste Bernadotte joined the French army in 1780 and was one of those who, like Napoleon Bonaparte, benefited hugely from the Revolution. In the army of Louis XVI one had to be well-born in order to obtain command; men of lesser social rank, however competent, were generally passed over. The Revolutionary armies, however, when called upon to defend what the new regime had achieved, needed men of talent. Bernadotte became an adjutant in 1790. France had to defend herself against all-comers in 1792, successfully at Valmy under Dumouriez, and by 1794 Bernadotte was general of a division. In 1795 he married Bernadine Eugénie Désirée Clary who had just been jilted, after a two-year affaire, by Napoleon. Her sister had already married Napoleon's brother, Joseph Bonaparte (the future, temporary, King of Spain).

Bernadotte disapproved of Napoleon's political ambition and opposed his establishment of the Consulate with himself as First Consul for life. Like many others, he felt that Napoleon had destroyed the hard-won Republic, that liberty, freedom of speech and conscience were fast disappearing. Bernadotte remained clear of plots against Napoleon, however; he served in numerous campaigns and became a Marshal of the Empire when his master made himself Emperor of the French. Still, he never liked Napoleon, thinking him far too over-bearing and personally arrogant; but though he might abstain from action against him, he was a persistent critic.

In 1810 Bernadotte's fortunes changed dramatically. King

Charles XIII of Sweden, desperate for an heir to his throne, met and liked Bernadotte, adopted him, and took him off to Sweden to train as his successor. Thereafter Bernadotte became Napoleon's avowed enemy and in 1813, when the previously vanquished Europeans rose against the Emperor, Bernadotte, now known as the Prince Royal of Sweden, personally led 100,000 Swedes and Russians against him. In the four-day battle at Leipzig in October of that year, 'the battle of the Nations', he and his men were instrumental in securing victory – the first time that Napoleon, fighting himself on the battle-field, had been defeated. Bernadotte became King of Sweden, founding a new dynasty part French, part Béarnais, and not at all Swedish. His old house in Pau, not unreasonably, is adorned with a Swedish flag.

# 5

## Lourdes, Gavarnie and St-Bertrand-de-Comminges

Nationale 117 goes, almost without deflection, to Tarbes. The only wriggle in its course occurs when it drops into the Adour valley, simultaneously crossing into the *département des Hautes-Pyrénées*, of which Tarbes is the capital. Its site on the left bank of the Adour caused its rise as a market-town, even in Roman times, but it also incurred attention from countless waves of destructive invaders, so that very little material fabric is left of its history. The cathedral, for example, was built in the twelfth century, but has been restored several times; nearby in Jardin Mussey a fifteenth-century cloister has been carefully rebuilt among the trees. Like Pau, however, Tarbes can be used as a centre for Pyrenean exploration: Belloc calls it 'the most truly Pyrenean town of all the plain . . . full of excellent entertainment'. It may still be so, but we were bound for Lourdes and the mountains again, so we left the N117 at Soumoulou, following a stream called Ousse. We crossed into *Hautes-Pyrénées* at Pontacq: the *département* is well-named, for along most of this section of the range the Pyrenees are impassable.

We parked in Lourdes near the Post Office, in the centre of a small square, where no payment was required between noon and 2 pm. Midday was fast approaching, so an early lunch at the palatial Café de la Poste nearby seemed a good idea.

Large miracles do not often occur; they may be prayed for at Lourdes, but are seldom granted. Many years ago I was on an expedition into the Pyrenees that went wrong. The weather was bad, I was on foot and camping, but conditions were so damp that my muscles were affected, and both legs became so sore and stiff that, as a Pyrenean walker in the Belloc and Morton stamp, I was a bad joke. Lourdes represented the farthest I knew I could possibly reach. With customary Anglo-Saxon scepticism, I had not even tried to pray for a cure for my muscular problems, had visited the basilica, seen the sights, and left next morning. I was on the way to Pau, and as I hobbled painfully out of Lourdes the distance there appeared to be of Siberian proportions. Almost at once a car stopped, and its young Spanish driver, who kept one of the Gospels taped to his dashboard, offered me a lift. He lived with his wife and family at Bordes, five miles from Pau. He showed me where his house was, but took me all the way into Pau. That was a small, but merciful, miracle.

The first miracle in Lourdes occurred in 1858, when, according to the New Roman Missal, 'the Blessed Virgin appeared eighteen times to Bernadette Soubirous, the fourteen-year-old shepherdess, in a grotto of the rock of Massabielle at Lourdes'.

The town had been of great importance before that. Standing on the point where the Gave de Pau emerges from its mountain valley, its high outcrop of rock afforded an ideal site for a defensive castle. Lourdes is in Bigorre, which shared Béarn's long and beneficial neutrality, so the castle which stands formidably upon the rock has no history of sieges.

Opposite the castle, over the river, a vast Religious City grew up around the rock of Massabielle. It contains three separate churches: the first, built in 1871, stands above the rock with a tall spire; the second is the crypt, beneath it; the third is a huge subterranean basilica, built in 1958 to mark the centenary of the apparition. This basilica is said to accommodate 20,000 people under its single, unsupported span of roof. Outside there is a

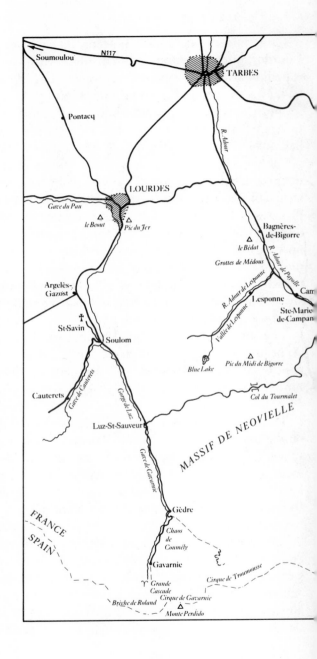

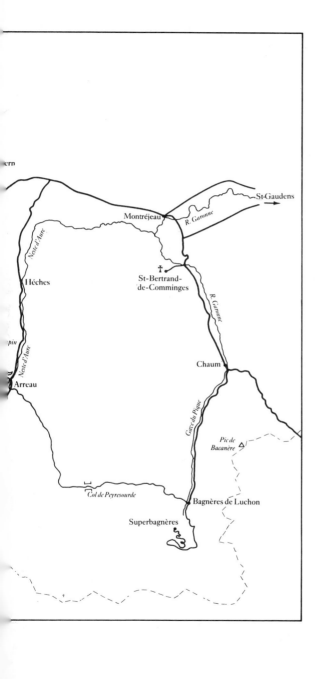

spacious esplanade for processions and outdoor services, with an immense statue of the Blessed Virgin. There are also two hospitals, of 700 beds apiece. Something in the region of three million pilgrims come to Lourdes every year, more than go to Rome or Mecca or any other pilgrim shrine in the world, and many of them require hospital care. When I was in Lourdes before, a massive congregation of people was gathered in the square in front of the basilica and a service was in progress, relayed by amplifier. All the galleries and staircases were packed, and in the space immediately in front were rank upon rank of people in invalid chairs; many more supported themselves on sticks and crutches. A fair proportion of the crowd were priests and nuns. As the priest officiating chanted, so the crowd responded, musically, repeating *'Vive Jésus, vive sa Croix.'* The expression of intense faith was moving, and faith is what originally built the whole extraordinary phenomenon.

Unfortunately, as Belloc, a Catholic himself, puts it, there is also 'that admixture of the supernatural which is invariably accompanied by detestable earthly adjuncts'. In the streets leading to the basilica and 'la Grotte', souvenir-shops stand side by side, facing each other across every roadway, all selling an identical collection of vulgar, tasteless and otherwise unsaleable curios and objects. They are very nearly rivalled in prolificacy by the hotels, but even so it is said that if you want to come to Lourdes in season (August and September are the peak months) you have to book early.

Earlier in the year, as we approached the confines of the Religious City, the wide esplanade was nearly empty, save for an occasional priest, nun or visitor. We climbed the ramped, winding approach to the crypt entrance and found on it the notice: 'If you are only here to visit, not to pray, stay out.' Fair enough, we stayed out. This crypt is the second basilica, called Basilica of the Rosary, and it incorporates the original grotto. What Bernadette's vision of the Virgin was telling her was where to find a spring of healing water: it is that which issues from the grotto, and what

St-Jean-de-Luz, the old harbour. In the centre, *Maison de l'Infante.*

*Left: Portal de Francia* and city walls, Pamplona.

*Below: Ayuntamiento* (town hall), Pamplona. From the second balcony the mayor announces the opening of Sanfermines.

*t: A trinitaire* in Gotein,
ée de Saison, Soule.

*w:* The monastery at
cesvalles, south of the pass.

*Above:* The church of Ste-Engrace, deep in the mountains. The churchyard is full of Basque marble gravestones.

*Left:* A group of Basques performing one of their ancient dances outside a gateway in the walls of St-Jean-Pied-de-Port.

*Opposite:* Pic du Midi d'Ossau, in the centre of the wildest country in all the Pyrenees.

Cirque de Gavarnie, a basin in the high mountains, where the Grande Cascade descends 1,300 feet.

*Opposite:* Pont-Napoléon, Luz-St-Sauveur, a single-span bridge crossing the Gave de Gavarnie on its way to Lourdes.

The Basilica at Lourdes, built over St Bernadette's Grotto.

St-Bertrand-de-Comminges: 'anyone who has poetry in his soul must go there'.

Pic du Midi de Bigorre: there is an orientation table and stupendous views of the whole Pyrenean landscape.

*Left:* Salardu, Val d'Aran, 'the Spanish Switzerland'.

*Below:* Parc Nacional de Aigues Tortes: the Enchanted Mountains, 'with high lakes where no footfall comes'.

'The extraordinary three-towered castle, the physical repository of Foix's history.'

Col de Puymorens, 6,282 feet, at the head of the Ariège.

*Left:* Mont-Louis, a milita[ry] stronghold to protect Fre[nch] property.

*Below:* Villefranche-de-Conflent, a mediaeval tow[n] fortified by Vauban.

The mighty Canigou, at 9,134 feet the last, going east, of the great Pyrenean peaks.

The Sardane, a Catalan dance: 'A step-dance, where the step changes in the middle of the bar, and beat changes in the middle of a step.'

*Left:* The abbey of St-Martin
du-Canigou, high up in the h
and silent as the tomb.

*Below:* The tribune in the chu
of the priory of Serrabone, an
education in the romanesque
style.

*Left:* The cathedral of Elne and its fine, romanesque cloister.

*Below:* 'The lovely romanesque porch of the abbey church of Santa Maria', Ripoll.

Calle de Santa Maria, Seo de Urgel, an ancient street in the oldest and most important bishopric in the Spanish Pyrenees.

thousands of the pilgrims come to drink. Of course, there are medicinal springs by the hundred all along the Pyrenees, but none other pin-pointed by divine intervention. The upper basilica is tall, with a high, soaring spire of some 230 feet, and as it was completed in 1871 it is well fenestrated and therefore much lighter than most French mediaeval churches. Every inch of it is covered in some kind of decoration.

If, out of the high pilgrim season, you choose to make Lourdes a centre for Pyrenean travels, there is much to recommend it. Apart from the castle, which has a splendid vantage point and a Musée Pyrénéen, there are the two peaks south of the town, Pic du Jer and Le Béout, from which the Gave emerges. Both can be reached by hill-climbing railways, and both give magnificent panoramic views of the mountains. In addition, about six miles west on the road to Pau that follows the Gave, are the Grottes de Bétharram, caves scoured out of the rock by an underground river, with weird limestone formations and all the thrills of a subterranean boat-trip.

There is Gavarnie, too, and that is our next objective. The valley of the Gave de Pau is now industrialized and fairly populous; the first place of any size is **Argelès-Gazost**, another watering-place but without the benefit of sanctity. Its sulphurous springs, as in other thermal stations throughout the Pyrenees, have brought dividends in the shape of an endless stream of ailing visitors, so it has squadrons of hotels to accommodate them. The scenery all around, of course, is superb, and there is a celebrated view of it from the Tour Mendaigne, in the upper part of the town.

A couple of miles up farther into the narrowing valley, at a place called Soulom, was a turning off to the right. We climbed steeply, above the busy valley road into lush green hillside pasture-land, to **St-Savin**. Perched high above the small village and the ground that descends sharply to the Gave, stands the abbey church that gave the village its name. All other traces of the abbey have disappeared, but the church is of the twelfth century and an unusual shape, cruciform but absidal, like a trefoil. The church may be locked out of season, as it was when we visited it, but if you can enter it, look out for the carved figure of Christ, by an anonymous Spanish wood-carver, of the same date as the church. The little abbey's patron saint is venerated as one of the apostles of the district of Lourdes. Legend has it that St-Savin was born in Barcelona, educated at Poitiers, became a Benedictine monk at Ligugé and finally a hermit, and died in about 820. Legend makes poor history: few of these statements can be substantiated.

At Soulom the valley bifurcates, with a stream coming in from a western valley called the Gave de Cauterets. **Cauterets** itself, five miles or so up the valley, is both a popular spa and a winter-sports centre, deep in the mountains, just the other side of the watershed, in fact, from the equally popular Balneario de Panticosa, both overlooked by the mighty Vignemale, of 10,820 feet. From the hillsides all round Cauterets come springs of sulphurous water, known from Roman times and believed in the sixteenth century to cure many ailments, including sterility in women. Queen Marguerite of Navarre, Henri II's wife, came here with her daughter, the Princess Jeanne d'Albret. There might be a small measure of uncertainty as to whether or not it was due to the waters of Cauterets, but in due course the princess was delivered of a baby boy, in that room in the Castle of Pau – 'Noustre Henric'.

The eastern valley at Soulom is the Gave de Gavarnie, tumbling through the very narrow Gorge de Luz, and climbing steeply up to **Luz – St-Sauveur**. This is another spa (few towns in the High Pyrenees are not) but it is really two towns, one on either side of the Gave. Both halves are well worth close inspection. St-Sauveur lies across the Pont Napoléon, a single-span bridge built in 1860 to commemorate the visit of Napoleon III and the Empress Eugénie, who came to St-Sauveur with their imperial court, so giving the little thermal station its finest hour. It is a pleasant, peaceful, elegant place, overlooking the deep valley of the Gave

*The church at Luz*

with splendid views of the high mountains beyond.

On the east bank of the Gave, back across Pont Napoléon, Luz is a bigger, busier town, with an attractive set of old houses around its square, and a very unusual fortified twelfth-century church in its centre. A high crenellated wall entirely surrounds the church, and you enter through a machicolated gatehouse: above the gate there is a projected overhang with holes in its base so that missiles could be directed vertically down on intruders. These walls were built in the fourteenth century; there is a small space between them and the church, doubtless so that the townspeople could seek refuge within this mini-fortress if Luz should come under attack. But from whom? Like Lourdes, Luz is in Bigorre and in the second half of the fourteenth century was brought under the protection of the famous Gaston Phoebus, Count of Foix-Béarn. He was certainly anxious to keep out his enemies, whether they were the forces of the Black Prince or those of his hated cousins, the Armagnacs. In fact he beat the Armagnacs at a place called Launac in 1362, and captured so many of their nobles and knights that he was able to raise large sums of money from their ransoms. I confess it is guesswork to connect the ransom money with the building of these walls at Luz, but he did certainly use ransom money to build defence-works elsewhere in his domains.

The church is plain and simple, typically romanesque with few windows, a semi-circular apse, and a lovely tympanum over the main door, showing Christ in Majesty flanked by the symbols of the four gospellers. Between the gatehouse and the church there are living quarters, perhaps for the priest, with a little outside stone staircase running up to the door. The buildings as a whole have a beautiful simplicity.

An interesting detour from Luz takes you to the **Col du Tourmalet**. The road there leads eastwards out of Luz, and winds around the southern slopes of the Pic du Midi de Bigorre, a mountain that stands out, apart from the watershed, north of the Massif de Néouvielle, a mountain wilderness of high peaks and hundreds of lakes. Although, says Belloc, the Pic du Midi is 'a bare mountain, all precipice upon the northern side, and steep every way', there is a road all the way up it and an observatory at the top, whence, on a clear day, there is a breathtaking view in all directions. The road from the pass then dips to the valley of the Adour at Ste-Marie-de-Campan.

At the end of this valley, though, is one of the highlights of the entire expedition, the famous Cirque de Gavarnie, dramatic enough in winter but seen to its best advantage when the snow has gone. There is a gap between the ski-ing and summer seasons when the hotels close, so be sure to check ahead if you are planning to travel in spring. Early in the season we had driven up the narrow course of the turbulent Gave through sleety rain, with towering, snowy, cloud-shrouded mountain masses rearing up on all sides. At Gèdre, a village high up in the precipitous valley, the snow had been thicker; a tortuous hairpin bend or two above it and the road wound higher still, through a rock-strewn wilderness aptly called Chaos de Coumély. At the end of it, at 4,452 feet, was Gavarnie, now famous as a ski-centre as well as for its Cirque. The hotels were shut and we had to return back through the unspeakable desolation of the Chaos, down the break-neck zig-zags to Gèdre. There, on the right of the road, was an establishment with an Alpine flavour in its architecture, called La Grotte. M. le Patron was a pleasant-looking man of young middle age. Asked if he had a room for the night he thought for a while, then said, 'No problem. Our rooms are normally for self-catering, you understand, but no problem. You can have one. Come this way.' Once the heating was turned on it was very comfortable, and the dining-room was beautiful: semi-circular, elegantly appointed, with an open fire in the corner, and candles on the tables. Monsieur offered us his own paté, to be followed by lamb chops 'from the mountain', cooked on the wood fire. It was a heavenly meal. Later he invited us to look at 'la Grotte' itself, through one of the glass doors at the rear of the restaurant, where there was a little balcony with tables and chairs. It overlooked a deep pool, and he switched some lights to show the rock cavern and its thundering cascade.

From La Grotte is a path that leads to **the Cirque de Troumousse** following the Gave de Héas, past the chapel, Notre-Dame de Héas. It is quite a climb but there is a beautiful view.

The real view, though, is the **Cirque de Gavarnie**. May is the earliest in the year you can be sure the snow will be gone, but June would be better, July better still. Flowers carpet the mountainsides, cow-bells and sheep-bells, bird-song and the music of water are the only sounds. The track starts from the top of the village, past the fourteenth-century Notre-Dame-des-Neiges, and a couple of hours' walk (you can hire a mule or donkey) brings you to a belvedere by the Pont de la Neige. Here is the Cirque de Gavarnie, a monstrous amphitheatre of towering grey mountains, several of them, like Monte Perdido, well over 10,000 feet high and all of them snow-capped all year round. These peaks are the watershed, the frontier, and on the other side they are in Spain. They are sheer granite rock, and from them come crashing thunderous cascades of icy water. One, the Grande Cascade, at over 1,300 feet, is the highest waterfall in

Europe. Not far away is a great gash in the mountain-wall, a cleft, like those in the Ste-Engrace valley, called the 'Brèche de Roland', because the mighty Roland himself made it with his stupendous sword, Durendal. Of course he did; everything is possible in these enchanted mountains.

We now took the road to **Bagnères-de-Bigorre**, back into hilly forest-land. As its name indicates, this is the kind of thermal station in which the waters are applied externally, rather than internally; it has a large and imposing bath-house. The town itself is pleasant, full of charming old houses in quiet streets, with a large Gothic-styled church of St-Vincent, which is surprising because it was built as late as the sixteenth century.

Bagnères-de-Bigorre is another excellent centre for exploring the Pyrenees. It stands on the Adour, the same Adour that swirls its broad waters into the sea beyond Bayonne, in a basin of the foothills of the mountains, a green amphitheatre leading the eye to their sterner, elder cousins on the white, serrated horizon. Close by Bagnères is the hill called le Bédat which might well have been purpose-built for a panoramic belvedere of the whole area. There are the Grottes de Médous, more subterranean caves like those at Bétharram, with a boat-trip through galleries of cunningly lit stalactites and stalagmites and mysterious shapes; and there is the valley of Lesponne, a mile farther south, where the Adour de Lesponne flows through a deep gorge from the Blue Lake, at an altitude of 6,378 feet, on the shoulder of the great Pic du Midi. In July, August and September there are excursions from the town to the mountain observatory with its orientation table and stupendous views of the whole Pyrenean landscape.

On the way out of town, up-valley, we called in at the Grottes de Médous, the subterranean river cave, and asked for tickets but were asked to wait for a party to assemble. How long might that be, we asked? *'On ne sait pas, Monsieur. Une demie-heure, peut-être.'* Or an hour, or the rest of the afternoon, if you are early in the season.

Off to the right the road leads to the Vallée de Lesponne. We headed for the **Col d'Aspin**. We drove through Campan and Ste-Marie-de-Campan, noticing that many of their houses and barns had crow-stepped gables, like those in Flanders and Holland. Even small cottages and cartsheds, cow-houses and tool-sheds were constructed in the same way, with flat stones rising to the apex of the gable. At Ste-Marie-de-Campan we took the left fork, following the Adour de Payolle. The road soon starts to climb, zig-zagging up through the trees and the village of Payolle to the snow-line and beyond it up to Col d'Aspin at 4,885 feet. Looming high on the right is the fearsome white head of l'Arbizon, and all around, lesser peaks showed their jagged teeth. At the Col, the view was exciting; row upon row of unidentifiable mountains, hundreds of them, all in shining crystal.

The road runs in neck-breaking hairpins into the bright green pastures of the Vallée d'Aure and its tiny, gabled villages. Arreau is a large village on the shallow Neste d'Aure, a good spot for anglers it seems. We followed the river down-valley, so narrow that cultivable land is scarce. At Hèches the river emerges from the hills, the landscape flattens, and there are various industrial works.

At La Barthe a delightful by-road follows the Neste on its way to join the Garonne, running through flat country, all arable fields, pasture for cattle and sheep, and greenwoods; from almost anywhere on this road you need only look to your right to see the endless range of white peaks rimming the horizon. At Montréjeau, where the Neste runs into the Garonne, take the road for Bagnères de Luchon, but before you reach Bagnères turn off right at Labroquère. You are near St-Bertrand-de-Comminges, and anyone who has poetry in his soul must go there. If you want a more direct route from Arreau, you can use the Col de Peyresourde.

**St-Bertrand-de-Comminges** stands up above the green Garonne plain, encircled by the mountains, its graceful cathedral soaring above ancient russet roofs and broken grey-stone walls. 'A city that is set on a hill cannot be hid.' We stopped the car and

*The cloisters at St-Bertrand-de-Comminges*

got out, to see it at this distance. The sun shone, making the pale walls reflect creamy light, against a background of green hills and clear, azure sky. We drove on up the winding road, first circling the walls then stopping at a terrace outside them where other sightseers were gathered. We made our way through the narrow streets of old houses, each one worth a poem and a painting, to the little square before the cathedral.

The way in to the cathedral is not through the great door beneath the tower, beneath the romanesque tympanum depicting the adoration of the Magi: one goes to the right, straight into the **cloisters**. The three sides are formed with columns of marble in pairs, their capitals carved in the most exquisite designs, of foliage, flowers, animals, scenes of the countryside; one of them bears the figures of the four evangelists, with their symbols. The cloisters were built on the former ramparts to the south of the cathedral, on an irregular square. As we strolled about, admiring the quiet beauty of these treasures and looking through the opening on the south side at the lovely Garonne landscape, the

104

mountains behind it, we could easily imagine the cathedral canons, for whom the cloisters were built, finding there in the warm sunshine the tranquility necessary for their contemplation.

The north side has great arches, because it is a vaulted passage outside the cathedral wall itself; it contains seven tombs of former canons, their families and benefactors. The cloisters were built, as was the first cathedral, in the early twelfth century. A door in the north passage leads into the cathedral, an amazingly light structure, which was built in three distinct phases.

This place was the country of the Convenae, one of the Nine Peoples, from whom the name Comminges is derived (as Bigorre is derived from the Bigerriones). In 72 BC, the Roman general Pompey, returning from a military expedition in Spain, found this little hill crowned with a small town, and saw in it a useful, strategically-sited base. He ordered the building of a Roman-style town adjacent to it. The remains of this, complete with forum, bath-house, theatre and temple, have been uncovered in the flat area below the hill, and some of the artefacts found there are in the town's museum. As Lugdunum Convenarum, this became a provincial capital, with a population of 50,000. The notorious King Herod was exiled there, not long after Christ's crucifixion. He was the youngest but most capable son of Herod the Great, King of Judaea, one of the Romans' 'client-kings' who were permitted to rule their subjects provided that they acknowledged Roman authority. Herod Antipas, this son, succeeded to part of his father's kingdom, including Galilee, and it appears that his rule was not unpopular. However, he was responsible for the death of St John the Baptist, and when Pontius Pilate, a notably undiplomatic governor of Judaea, tried to pass on Jesus, as a Galilean, to him for trial, Herod refused, not wanting to be involved. Both these gentlemen were removed from office as a consequence of the disorder caused by the Crucifixion.

In AD 409, when the Western Empire was being overrun by the Germanic tribes from across Rhine and Danube, the Vandals arrived in Aquitania and wiped out the lower, Roman town; the survivors took refuge behind the walls of the old *oppidum* on the hill. Despite their troubles, the Convenae built there the first Christian basilica, where some of their sarcophagi have been found. Unfortunately, this stage of the town's life ended in 585, when Gontran, King of the Burgundians (another of the barbarian tribes from Germany) completely destroyed it. Lugdunum Convenarum just ceased to exist.

The hilltop site remained deserted for five hundred years until 1073, when Bertrand de l'Isle arrived on the scene. A canon of Toulouse and son of a noble family, he had just been created bishop of the rural diocese of Comminges. He visited the deserted hilltop, saw its possibilities and began the building of his diocesan cathedral there. It was a miniature episcopal city. The work was finished in the early twelfth century: the cloister, the doorway with its tympanum in the tower, the narthex, the very short ante-nave (all that was necessary for the lay congregation) and the walls along the south side of the choir. Bertrand was canonized in 1218 for his virtuous life and his work, particularly his recognition of the value of the local thermal waters and their curative effect, and the little city took the name of St-Bertrand-de-Comminges.

The tomb of St Bertrand attracted pilgrims, and by the end of the thirteenth century another Bishop Bertrand thought it necessary to enlarge the cathedral to accommodate the flow of pilgrims. When he was made archbishop of Bordeaux in 1304, he nevertheless returned to St-Bertrand and laid the first stone of a massive Gothic nave, the work to be completed by the canon-sacrist, Adhemar de St-Pastou. In 1309 Archbishop Bertrand became the first of the Avignon popes, Clement V, but continued as patron for the Comminges cathedral.

The **cathedral** nave is high and light, with a clerestory of windows, all coloured, and a semi-circle of windows in the apse. When the sun streams in, diffusing the subtle colours in patterns within the pale stone walls, the cathedral becomes a wondrous aurora, in which visitors can only stand still and marvel.

An additional chapel was added on the north of the nave by Bishop Hughes de Chatillon, starting about 1350 and finished in the early fifteenth century, in flamboyant Gothic. A little later Bishop Pierre de Foix rebuilt the shrine of St Bertrand, to which his remains were transferred eventually in 1476.

Finally, Bishop Jean de Mauléon, in the mid-sixteenth century, built in the centre of the Gothic nave the magnificent carved wooden **choir**. He inaugurated its building on Christmas night 1535, and brought to it all the artistic skills of the Italian Renaissance, but without abandoning the symbolism of the Middle Ages. There are 66 choir stalls, all exquisitely carved in high and low-relief, half-relief and marquetry, 'one of the purest joys of the French Renaissance'. The themes, decorating, it seems, every square inch of the polished wood, also vary, from proper religious subjects, such as the Virgin, the saints, the Christian Fathers, virtues, prophets and so on, to mythological, allegorical and even faintly scatological designs. The choir-stalls were for the canons, who were expected to sing their offices and chant their liturgy without being seen by the lay congregation, penned in the little nave. The latter, in addition to being somewhat detached from the centre of the service, also had to contend with the sepulchral tones of the massive organ, situated in their midst. This monumental instrument occupies an entire corner of the nave, from floor to ceiling, wonderfully ornamented and carved, oddly enough, with lay rather than ecclesiastical subjects, and is contemporary with the wooden choir-stalls. The organ is known as 'the third marvel of Gascony', the first being the windows of Auch, the second, the bell-peal of Rieux. It has, of course, needed repair and restoration, but has only received three complete overhauls in its 440-year existence. At the time when we wandered around the choir, wondering at the skill of the carvers, it constituted a class-room for a large group of woolly-hatted children, being taught eloquently about their present surroundings by their master.

The bell-tower is at the extreme west end of the cathedral, and one goes through its base to leave. Like many a mediaeval church, this one had to be fortified, and the tower looks more like a castle keep than a bell-tower; in fact, it is referred to as the donjon. It is high, about 108 feet, and topped with a shallow-pitched, tiled roof of four triangles.

The survival of this wonder of the Pyrenees is largely due to sheer luck: it happened not to be in the way of any of the conflicts which affected other regions, save for a serious outbreak of violence during the so-called 'religious' wars of the late sixteenth century; Christian against Christian. Even the Revolution spared the cathedral, although it removed the bishop despite objections raised by his flock, who pointed out that they, as townsmen, owed their living to the bishop and his chapter. The Convention changed the town name to Hauteville but, as in St-Jean-de-Luz, the people changed it back again as soon as possible.

The old stone houses in the little square by the west door, the fountain in the centre, the gentle afternoon sunshine warming the russet tiles and pale stone; the little town, encircled within its old walls, plays the essential accompaniment, quietly and effectively, to the supreme virtuosity of the soloist. In one visit to St-Bertrand-de-Comminges you can learn a history of man's achievement in art-forms; you can undergo a moving spiritual experience; you can leave the modern world of relentless noise and financial anxieties, and enter a kind of earthly paradise, where nothing matters except the warmth of the sun, the beauty of old achievements, and the sublime serenity of the mountain country.

The appointed exit route winds through one of the ancient gateways in the walls and down again to the river-plain, where we traced a way through country lanes, among the cattle-pastures and fields of wheat and maize, to the valley road following the Garonne upstream, once more into the mountains: dead ahead was the mass of Pic de Bacanère. At Chaum the road splits, the left fork going across the Garonne and chasing it up Val d'Aran, in Spain, the right, skirting the western flank of the Pic alongside a tributary to the Garonne called the Pique, to **Bagnères de Luchon**. The railway, accompanying road and river, comes to its terminus there, and stately villas appear in tree-lined avenues.

# 6

# The Val d'Aran:
# from Luchon to Foix and Tarascon

We opted to stay at a simple hotel-bar-restaurant called 'Le Faison d'Or'. Drinks were served in the little bar, a small room with well-used wooden furniture where several worthies were in for aperitifs and four young men were playing cards. They made a good deal of noise about it but we enjoyed the atmosphere: it was totally different from the classy Café de la Coupole in Pau but also typically French, a spit-and-sawdust kind of place, unsophisticated, functional but still imbued with the spirit of civilization. The dining-room had one long table down the middle, so we assumed that the people at it were of the same family party, though there was no conversation between the two ends. Three of the card-players came in to eat; nothing exotic, just good victuals, well cooked. The family at our end of the long table finally left, and the family at the other end stayed to gossip about them with Madame la Patronne.

The wide main street, the Allées d'Etigny, leads to the Parc des Quinconces at its southern end, where the old bath-house, built in 1858, now houses the town museum; the new baths stand at right angles to it. In the square there is a band-stand, trees and flowers, and hotels; the whole reminded us of Harrogate, or Bath.

There is also a statue of Baron d'Etigny, who established the town as a popular health resort in the eighteenth century but, as with so many of these spas, the Romans had been there first. Nearby is a relatively small subsidiary mountain with a ski-resort called Superbagnères. You can get to it by road or rack-and-pinion railway, and there is a splendid mountain-view from the top. This is the mountain from which the hot, sulphurous waters spring, and the Romans first attested to their health-giving quality. They can be used in the treatment of rheumatism and respiratory problems, and anyone who uses the voice for a living, whether opera singer, actor or barrister, can marinate his or her vocal chords in them when in need of resuscitation.

Luchon, as it is generally called, is deep in the mountains, and its valley of the Pique is a dead-end. Beyond it lies the Spanish frontier, inaccessible because of the massive mountain chain of Maladeta, which includes the biggest and noblest of them all, the great Néthou (Aneto in Spanish), which is 11,181 feet high. Luchon is therefore the most truly Pyrenean of all the resorts, health, winter-sports or holiday, and a fine town as well, with plenty of good hotels (as well as the more modest kind like ours), a casino, the baths, the museum and access to any number of mountain walks.

From here you can visit one of the anomalies of the Pyrenees, the variously spelt Val d'Aran, Vall d'Aran or Valle de Aran. The word Aran is Basque, meaning valley, but Basques have never been known to live here except, presumably, in the unrecorded, pre-historic past. It lies in the geographical fault in the Pyrenees chain, between the two axes of the watershed. Deep in its hills springs the great Garonne, one of the foremost rivers of France, yet with its source in Spain. Clearly, Aran ought to be in France, geographically, and its people, up to twenty years ago, still spoke a dialect, called *aranes*, of the local Comminges *patois*, the Gascon of south-western France. There is at the head of the valley a pass into Spain, called Bonaigua, but it is a very long journey, down the course of the river Noguera Pallaresa, before you get to a town of any size. There is also a tunnel, opened in 1955, under the mountains from Viella, the capital of Aran, down the valley of the

Noguera Ribagorzana, but again many difficult miles lie ahead before reaching Lerida on the Segre. The tunnel, I am told, is only two-way, and very dark, which does not give the motorist much pleasure.

As a kind of no-man's land, Aran governed itself, like most of the isolated valleys on the Spanish side of the Pyrenees, but remained a bone of not very enthusiastic contention between authorities in France and Spain until 1659. Until 1192 it had belonged to the county of Comminges. Thereafter sovereignty remained vague and uncertain: because the Pass of Bonaigua was easier of access than the narrow and dangerous gorge through which the Garonne thunders down to its lower course, Spain tended to exert more influence than France.

In 1659, however, Louis XIII concluded the Treaty of the Pyrenees with his erstwhile brother-in-law, Philip IV of Spain, on the little Isle of Pheasants in the Bidassoa. In principle the frontier would follow the watershed, but what about the gap between the two watersheds? The court officials conducting the negotiations on the French side had little actual knowledge of the mountains and their vagaries. 'The Val d'Aran,' said the Spanish negotiators casually, 'of course you regard as Spanish.' To which the French, to whom the name meant about as much as would some Armenian enclave in the Caucasus, replied 'Of course,' and the matter was concluded for ever.

To reach this outpost of Spain, leave Luchon on the down-valley road, past the railway terminus, and along the tumbling Pique. It skirts the cloudy flanks of Bacanère and comes to the little manufacturing village of Cierp, near where the Pique projects itself into the Garonne. Turning right here, there are dark, dank quarries at Marignac, then the Garonne is reached at St-Béat, turning right on the main road and into a deep rocky cleft in the looming mountains. The river thrusts through the narrow rocks, tumultuous and strong, crashing down on its long, long course to the Atlantic Ocean. It is as well not to make this trip, as we did, on a Sunday. At Melles we were surprised to join the tail

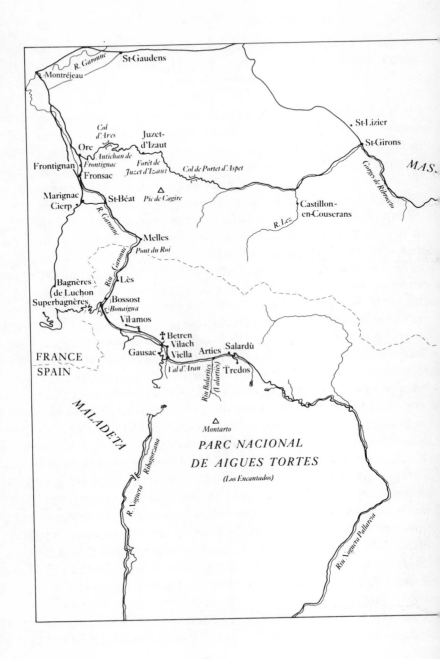

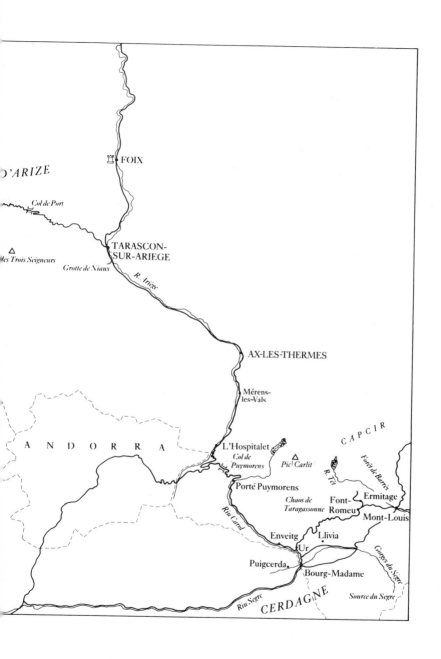

D'ARIZE

Col de Port

△
les Trois Seigneurs

🏰 FOIX

TARASCON-
SUR-ARIEGE

Grotte de Niaux

R. Ariège

AX-LES-THERMES

Mérens-
les-Vals

ANDORRA

CAPCIR

L'Hospitalet

Col de
Puymorens

Pic Carlit △

Forêt de Barrès

R. Tet

Porté Puymorens

Chaos de
Taragassonne

Font-
Romeu

Ermitage

Mont-Louis

Riu Carol

Enveitg

Llivia

Ur

Gorges du Sègre

Puigcerda

Bourg-Madame

Riu Segre

CERDAGNE

Source du Segre

of a long string of cars waiting to pass through the frontier checkpoint: all of France appeared to be joining us on this jaunt into Spain. A little farther on and you cross the Garonne by the Pont du Roi and enter Spanish **Aran**.

It is best to see the valley from the top, just below the Pass of Bonaigua, to the bottom. There are seven large villages in Aran, and 23 hamlets. The seven, from the top, are Salardu, Arties, Viella, Vilach, Vilamos, Bossost and Lès. Viella is the capital, although Vilach and Vilamos were more important in the Middle Ages, and Vilamos is the oldest settlement of all. The Garonne, here called Garona de Ruda, comes into the valley at its head, from the wild mountains to the south. Officially, this area of the mountains, of high peaks, deep ravines and countless lakes, is called Parc Nacional de Aigues Tortes. It is also called 'Los Encantados', the Enchanted Mountains, and the most experienced and intrepid of mountain walkers have been reduced to quivering nervous wrecks by encounters with them. Even J. B. Morton, as hardy as any, writes in his *Pyrenean* of 'those terrible mountains called the Encantados, eight and nine thousand feet of jumbled rock, with high lakes where no footfall comes, and enormous chasms brimmed with mist, and torrents that plunge from inaccessible cliffs and fill the air with ice-cold spray . . .' He confesses to fear, rising to blind panic, at the prospect of losing his way up there, blundering frantically about until a false step might plunge him into one of those frightful abysses. 'Nobody,' he says, 'would ever go there for pleasure.'

So much for the impenetrable barrier south of Aran. The first hamlet below Bonaigua is Tredos, at 4,500 feet, where there is a twelfth-century church (locked), standing up high over the valley. A mile farther down the road – which is nowadays wide and easy – and set above it with a sweeping zig-zag to reach it, is Salardu, chief town of the upper valley, reached through a thirteenth-century gateway. Another short distance, steadily losing height, and there is **Arties**. In Basque, Arties means 'between two waters', which describes its position accurately enough, because it is here that the Garonne is joined by a tributary called Valarties (in Spanish, Balaritas). The name indicates the antiquity of the settlement, coming as it does from pre-history. The view up the Valarties frames the peak Montarto, a 9,000-foot monster marking the fringe of the enchanted wilderness. From the main road one may also see two buildings on the right bank of the Garonne, apart from the village. One is a disused church of the thirteenth century which once belonged to the Knights Templar; the other is Casa Portola, a fortified manor-house of the sixteenth century. A short way downstream from Arties stand the Thermal baths, rather less well-known, it seems, than those of Luchon, but no doubt just as efficacious.

This part of the valley is known locally as Mig Aran, (pronounced meech) which means middle. At Betren, a short way from Viella, you can see the romanesque church of San Esteban, which has a good tympanum over the main door. Twenty years ago **Viella** had a population below a thousand, just one petrol pump, and every drink cost one peseta, according to Henry Myhill in his excellent *The Spanish Pyrenees*. Eighteen years ago I went into several Pyrenean bars on the Spanish side, along the Bidassoa and Baztan. They tended to be merely a part of a village store: at one end little girls were buying bread and eggs, and at the other Basque-speaking elders were discussing the price of sheep (or something like that) and scruffy vagabonds like myself could ask for a drink without being treated to the curled lip displayed by barmen in more pretentious establishments. All one had to do was slap a peseta piece on the zinc, say *'Un tinto, por favor,'* and the gentleman who served all would produce a small glass and fill it with good, rough, red wine. 'Mais où sont les neiges d'antan?'

Viella, as the capital of Aran, is the seat of local government; such items as the land registry may be found here instead of in the distant provincial capital of Lerida. There are some good houses here too, some of the seventeenth century, belonging to substantial Aran families. The **church** is twelfth-century romanesque, with some circular windows and others small, high and round-arched in the Roman fashion. There is a small but good tympanum over the door, which is beneath the octagonal tower, and a later cupola over the chancel, with two transepts, both with highly ornate gilded altars. Its most celebrated feature is a fragment of sculpture, in a glass case, labelled 'Ecce homo' and known as 'the Christ of Mig Aran'. A notice by it claims, in Spanish, that it is 'considered the greatest and most dramatic of the romanesque Christs in the Pyrenees'.

There is in the vicinity of Viella a menhir, a pre-historic standing stone, known as Peira de Mig Aran, which in those times had pagan religious significance for the central part of the valley. Facing it across the river is the hamlet Gausac, with the only Gothic church in the whole valley. These little hamlets are dotted all the way down this part of the valley as far as Bossost, which is quite large and boasts another twelfth-century romanesque church with a tympanum worth seeing. Tradition says the people of Bossost vowed that if they were spared the ravages of the notorious Black Death, in the mid-fourteenth century, they would build seven chapels. They were, and they did: in fact they went one better – there are eight little *ermitas*.

Lès is the last village, which possibly derives its name from the Roman god Lex; there are relics of a Roman bath-house, with an inscription to him.

Aran is known in Spain as 'the Spanish Switzerland', both for its mountain scenery and for an abundance of milk cows, some of Swiss stock. As far as we could see, there is another way in which this comparison is apt, and that is its capacity to absorb and cater for tourists. Every village has an outer growth of hotels and holiday apartment-blocks, with many more building. Winter sport is today big business, and this is what most tourists come for, rather than the scenery or places of historical interest. The economy of the Aranese, therefore, no longer depends on milk, butter and cheese. There is also the fact that some goods cost less in Spain than they do in France and can also be bought on Sundays, hence the lines of cars waiting to cross the border.

116

Leaving Luchon we drove northward along the Pique, heading for the country north of Val d'Aran where a spur of the mountains separates the territory of the Convenae from that of the Consevanni, the last of the identifiable Nine Peoples. The district is still called Couserans, and its capital is St-Girons.

We crossed the Garonne a little below the point where it is joined by the Pique, and turned left. No more main roads. You are in for a feast of little winding lanes and pure, unadulterated Pyrenean landscape. You may enjoy the very narrow streets of Frontignan and Ore, between ancient, grey-walled, pantiled houses, all hanging precariously on the steep hillside. The road zig-zags quickly up to the still more vertiginously-sited Antichan-de-Frontignes, and soon you are over **Col des Ares**, looking down on the shining green valleys and their russet-tiled villages. From the other side, above the tiny village Moncaup, we stopped and got out, revelling in the view down-valley towards the forest of Juzet d'Izaut on the slopes of Pic de Cagire. We were alone on the road, and as we stood in the warmth of the sun we could bask in the absolute tranquility of the mountains, the silence that filled, as we listened, with birdsong, animal sounds, streams rippling, nothing that was not natural. Below, we could see a Moka van winding along the lane from Arguenos to Moncaup, delivering ice-cream to Moncaup's café. From the forest came the buzzing of a *tronconneuse*, like a distraught bluebottle. A hawk hung motionless above the trees, a blackbird carolled lustily from a nearby silver birch; Brimstone and Orange-tip butterflies settled momentarily on the spring flowers of the mountainside.

This seductive Arcady could have held us for much longer. We drove down its narrow lanes at no great rate, through the comatose Juzet d'Izaut, spellbound like Ste-Engrace in some kind of mediaeval trance, into the forest and up by marvellously twisting loops to **Col de Portet d'Aspet**. A hundred feet or so below the pass we came to a complete stop; the council men were there with their lorries, their hydraulically movable platforms and their *tronconneuses*, lopping off the foliage that overhung the road, apparently a regular hazard. 'Wait there for a while,' said one burly, moustachioed hero in *ouvrier-bleu* overalls; space was made and we eased past, not looking too closely at the dizzy drop within inches of our offside wheels. Up on the col, at 3,500 feet, with the village of Portet d'Aspet tucked into the slope just below it, was another idyllic green prospect: the country of the Consevanni, fringed to the south by lofty white peaks.

We were following the course of the little river Bouigane, now, and villages thronged its banks every mile or so. Clearly the valley was fertile or it would never have supported so many people, but today the principal activity seems to be logging, and the essential form of draught on the steep hillsides was horses. Here was a Pyrenean landscape in a natural setting, relying on a natural economy, its communities living in their patrimonial houses of stone with few modern additions, undisturbed by the ugly accretions of tourism or the ski-industry.

At Audressein the Bouigane joins the Lez, a short way downstream from Castillon-en-Couserans, and the road follows it along its valley to the Salat and the town of St-Girons.

As a small local capital, St-Girons is not too exciting. The Salat pours over a weir near the bridge, there are splendid views of the mountains to the south, and there are paper-making factories, but there is not much more to tell of it. Warm sunshine gave us the opportunity to lunch at a pavement café in a street typically French, with tall shuttered houses, their balconies vividly overflowing with flowers, and an air of artlessness that contrasted pleasantly with some of the more tourist-conscious towns. You may wish to sample the local wine: the eighteenth-century farmer-traveller, Arthur Young, admired it. Around the Pyrenees, in fact, there are many local wines, and all those we tasted proved good.

The early capital of the Consevanni was at St-Lizier, a mile or so to the north, which takes its name from a sixth-century saint called Glycerius. It is still the diocesan centre and has a

118

twelfth-century, romanesque cathedral with a two-storey cloister and a wealth of decorated capitals.

The Salat at St-Girons draws its waters from many Pyrenean streams, which in Comminges and here in Couserans are not called Gaves but *rivières,* as in any other part of France but Béarn. If you want to go to Foix directly you can drive straight along N117, about 25 miles, but it is more interesting to trace one of the streams, the Arac, by taking a road that follows it through a spur of the mountains, the Massif de l'Arize, where it cuts a deep trench, the Gorges de Ribaouto. The landscape is superb: at Massat you turn a sharp right-angle and begin to climb, in the usual circuitous fashion, high into the hills to the Col de Port, 4,100 feet and snow-covered. To the right, Pic des Trois Seigneurs peers over the tops of lesser heights; before us the road dipped into a distant green valley, and on the horizon stood the range that forms the northern frontier of Andorra, like a row of gleaming white sharks' teeth. It was a magnificent sight.

The road descended swiftly, in great swooping loops to the trees and pastures. I am sure I saw a Camberwell Beauty butterfly on the way. I have never seen one in England, but years ago I saw two in Provence, and this was the first since then.

The countryside you see from the Col de Port belongs to the County of Foix, which is based on the valley of the Ariège. The road reaches the river just north of Tarascon, and a pleasant lane on its left bank leads into the town of **Foix**. The town's centre is the market place, and the market was in full swing, with stalls selling everything, clothes, shoes, books and every conceivable type of paraphernalia, and covered halls for food-marketing. Over all loomed the extraordinary three-towered castle, the physical repository of Foix's history. The first fortification built on this obviously defensible site, a rocky eminence guarding the passage of the Ariège as it skirts the Massif de l'Arize, dates from 1012 and was built by the viscount of Carcassonne for his son, who then declared himself count of Foix.

Dukes and counts were originally appointed in France by

Charlemagne and his immediate successors, to administer certain districts. The terms were borrowed from the later Roman Empire and were both military ranks. *Dux* was a commander of frontier troops; *comes* (literally, companion of the emperor) was a general officer commanding a field army. Charlemagne and his dynasty, the 'Carolingians', gave much to their faithful servants and they and their issue took more, by force of arms or personality, or both. In theory the dukes and counts were merely royal appointments, not transferable by heredity, but the Franks were not like the Romans of old, used to central government and regular administration. They were Germanic, subject to strict family traditions: as Tacitus said of them; 'a man's heirs and successors are his own children, and there is no such thing as a will'. Once royal power had bestowed a title and lands on any Frank, there was no question of handing it all over to someone else. They all began little dynasties, ruling over their little territories. The farther their territory was from the king, the more independent the counts and viscounts could feel themselves to be. The duchy of Aquitaine was vast and many of its lands were virtually inaccessible, protected by mountains and impregnable fortresses like this of Foix. Control of Charlemagne's vast dominions quickly slipped out of his son's and his grandsons' hands, and this county of Foix, like the viscounty of Béarn, continued to be more or less autonomous throughout a large part of the Middle Ages, its independence only threatened when it attracted royal attention.

The Aquitanians seem to have had a tendency to independence in religious thought as well as political. They embraced Calvin's theories in Béarn and they were also heavily involved in the so-called Albigensian heresy in the early thirteenth century, and in the savage 'crusade' to extirpate it. The heresy was a form of dualism and arose at least partly because of the poor quality of the priests and bishops whose duty it was to expound the Christian faith to their flocks, and who could not even read enough Latin to translate the Bible to them. A sharp distinction between good and evil led men to believe that only by extreme ascetism could one's soul be made pure enough to enter the Kingdom of Heaven. Those who tried, and were known as *perfecti*, were prohibited marriage and the eating of meat (because it was believed that animals had souls). They led a life so pure they were called Cathars, from the Greek word *catharos*, meaning pure, and were accorded unstinting admiration by the mass of believers who could not attempt such perfection. When their heresy was brought to the attention of the great Pope Innocent III, and he had grasped that the *perfecti* believed they were entitled to a place in Heaven, not by God's grace but by their hard-earned right, he dispatched three Cistercian abbots to the area with the commission of explaining to the heretics the error of their ways. They were unsuccessful because, as an Augustinian canon from Spain called Dominic pointed out, they were accompanied by all the trappings of their important station, and the pomposity of their retinue was precisely the aspect of the Church that the Cathars believed was totally wrong. The said Dominic later formulated a different kind of priesthood who could appear, like Christ's apostles, without the sin of pride, among people poor as themselves, and stand a better chance of persuading them out of their mistaken doctrines: they came to be known as Dominican friars.

In the meantime the heresy raged unabated. so the Pope resorted to military persuasion. Northern knights, delighted at the opportunity to ransack the more affluent south, flocked to join this 'crusade', and performed such unspeakable atrocities that the heresy had little chance of survival. Nor did its practitioners. The heretics were called Albigensians because their centre was Albi, but they inhabited many of the towns and villages of the Toulousain, Foix and Roussillon. This great castle of Foix withstood repeated attacks by the crusaders, under Simon de Montfort, the father of the man who inherited the earldom of Leicester and played a leading part in thirteenth-century English politics. The northern knights devastated the wealthy south and robbed it of many of its treasures, but it took 40 years finally to subdue the heretics. Up in the hills, south-east of Foix and due south of Lavelanet, at a height of nearly 4,000 feet, stand the ruins of the castle of **Montségur**, and it was here that the last act in the grim tragedy was played. The remaining heretics were besieged for six months, in 1244. Finally they were forced to surrender. Some 200 of them had survived and all were burnt at the stake.

The castle of Foix also surrendered, 28 years later, but for a different reason. Count Roger-Bernard III of Foix had refused homage to King Philip III of France, and the latter was not one to take such obduracy lying down. His sappers started to dig out the rock at the foot of the castle, which alarmed the garrison sufficiently to cause them to submit. This contumacious count was a contemporary of the equally disobedient Viscount Gaston VII of Béarn, who refused homage to King Edward I of England, and paid for that with a spell in Winchester prison. He later married one of his daughters to Roger-Bernard, so that when Gaston died without a male heir in 1290, Foix and Béarn united, to the rage of another of Gaston's sons-in-law, the count of Armagnac, who coveted Béarn himself.

Souvenir-shops in Foix are full of postcards, pictures and models featuring a tall, blond gentleman in knightly garb, brandishing a sword and labelled Gaston Fébus. This is Count Gaston III, called Phoebus, of Foix-Béarn, and Foix is as proud of him as Pau.

Gaston Phoebus ruled his domains as an autocrat: that was the only feasible way of making his wishes effective, because if he called any of the various legislative assemblies, his *Cour Majour*, the *Cour des barons*, or the *Cour des Communautés*, he usually ended up by having to grant them fresh privileges at the expense both of his own power and that of the majority of his poorer subjects. If he wished to overhaul the administration of his estates he would have to dispense with the courts, and he did. He replaced them with a Privy Council, without a fixed composition but usually consisting of his relatively few functionaries, recruited either from members of his own family or from the more competent and honest of the townsmen. This policy certainly enabled a much more efficient and equitable government of Foix, Béarn and all his other territories, but it also precipitated a dangerous plot against him by those who had been squeezed out of power. Gaston's own son, the heir to the county, was persuaded to join the plotters in an attempt to poison his father. It was found out, and Gaston was understandably enraged, especially by his son's involvement. He called to his castle at Orthez in Béarn a council of all the barons and prelates of Foix and Béarn, and told them he intended to put his son to death. They protested, since there was no other heir, so Gaston decided merely to punish him with a month or two's imprisonment, then send him away on a long journey.

The young man was duly incarcerated, but refused to eat. 'On hearing this,' says Jean Froissart, the chronicler, 'the Count grew very angry and left his room without a word to go to the tower. As ill luck would have it, he was holding a little knife with which he pared his nails. He had the prison door opened and went up to his son, holding the knife by the blade near the point – so near it, indeed, that the part which stuck out beyond his fingers was no longer than the thickness of a Tours shilling. By an evil chance, when he thrust that tiny point against his son's throat, saying, "Ha, traitor, why don't you eat?" he wounded him in some vein.

'The Count came away immediately, without saying or doing anything more, and went back to his room. The young man's blood had run cold with fear at the sight of his father, and in addition he was weak with fasting when he saw or felt the point of the knife pricking his throat. Lightly though it did so, it was in a vein. He turned his face away and died there and then.'

This tragedy, which occurred in the tall, bleak and grim tower of the castle of Orthez, came as a stain on the otherwise shining character of Gaston Phoebus. Froissart bears out the pride in him still taken by the twentieth-century citizens of Foix.

'At the time when I was with him,' he writes, 'Count Gaston of

Foix was about fifty-nine. I can say that, though I have seen many knights, kings, princes and others in my life, I have never seen one who was so finely built, with better-proportioned limbs and body or so handsome a face, cheerful and smiling, with eyes which sparkled amiably when he was pleased to look at anyone. He was so accomplished in every way that it would be impossible to praise him too highly. He loved everything which it was right to love and hated whatever deserved hatred. He was a shrewd nobleman, bold in action and sound in judgement.'

Gaston died in 1391, after a hunting expedition.

At the top of the market place there is a terrace, a small fountain and a bust of the composer Gabriel Fauré. Fauré was not a native of Foix, he was born in 1845 in the smaller town of Pamiers, some fourteen miles north of Foix on the N20. His father was superintendent of schools there, but although Gabriel spent his early days in Pamiers he was sent at the age of nine to Paris, as he had won a scholarship to the École Niedermeyer, a school for the education of church musicians; he was a school-fellow of Camille Saint-Saens. Fauré eventually became Professor of Composition at the Paris Conservatoire in 1896, but by that time his major works had been written. He never tackled opera or symphonies, but his songs were reckoned masterpieces of their genre, and he is best known for his setting of Verlaine's poems to music in the song cycle 'La Bonne Chanson' (1892), and most of all for his 'Requiem' of 1887. He died in Paris in 1924.

Toward the sheer rock of the castle the streets wind in anarchic complexity, lined narrowly with houses of stone, or half-timbered and jettied. We found our way to a little square before the old **Cathedral of St Volusien**. It is twelfth-century in origin, standing on the site of an abbey which was built over the grave of St Volusien. This worthy was an archbishop of Tours, martyred on the spot in 497, presumably by one or other of the barbarian hordes, Vandals, Visigoths or Franks. Judging by the outside of the church, it was probably the Vandals, and their tradition has passed on: I have seldom seen an exterior so scarred, battered, delapidated and neglected. Some of the bushes growing out of the masonry were quite large. The square tower appears never to have been finished, but there is a good romanesque doorway. Inside the cathedral is high, cool, and quite light, since it was heightened, and extended with an apse, in the fifteenth century, when the choir-stalls were added.

Foix is a provincial capital, not a holiday resort, so it has few hotels, restaurants or other tourist amenities, and for those reasons if for none other, is highly commendable. There is, however, one attractive feature in the locality well worth visiting, and that is the underground river of Labouiche. You may reach it by the road leading north from the castle, turning left at Vernajoul; it is three miles altogether from Foix. You can take a boat and travel a mile through caverns with amazing limestone formations. We eventually took the main road up the Ariège valley, the Nationale 20, and were soon in **Tarascon**. From our balcony in the Hostellerie de la Poste we could not only see the Ariège hurrying past just below the hotel's terraces, but the mountains at its back, presiding over the green plain.

Tarascon-sur-Ariège is another of the many Pyrenean towns which could provide a base from which to explore the mountains. It has a lovely riverside situation, a little hill with a watchtower, Tour St-Michel, close behind it, and just across the river is its church, fourteenth-century like the tower, with a fine doorway. A mile or so along the road which goes to Vicdessos, deep in the hills, is a cavern called Grotte de Niaux, with prehistoric wall-paintings. Furthermore the Nationale 20 will take you to Ax-les-Thermes, the Puymorens Pass into the Cerdagne, and the fearful Embalire into Andorra. The only thing that we could find wrong with Tarascon was a neighbouring dog, which chose to bark at hours when all sensible dogs are asleep.

# 7

# The Cerdagne and the Massif du Canigou

We drove along the wide Ariège valley-road between towering hills that crowded road, railway and river together closely, leaving hardly room enough for arable land and villages; yet of villages there were plenty. **Ax-les-Thermes** has spread into some of its suburban villages because, like Bagnères-de-Luchon, it is now a winter-sports centre as well as an ancient health resort, and has therefore added substantially to its capacity for making money.

The waters of Ax issue from over 60 springs of varying temperatures. The name Ax, like Aix-en-Provence, is from Aquae, telling us that once again the Romans were here first. These waters are apparently beneficial, particularly to sufferers from respiratory complaints. They were at one time evidently thought to be helpful to lepers, too. In Place du Breilh is a hospital, and in front of the hospital a fountain called 'Bassin des Ladres'. According to tradition the sainted King Louis IX of France had it put there in the thirteenth century, for the benefit of returning leprous crusaders.

Ax today is a thriving town: there is a big new hotel, the thermal establishments, and a casino which is said to have a cosmopolitan and almost family atmosphere. Winter sports form a strong element in its attractions, but summer visitors will find that there are wonderful mountain walks to be enjoyed in all directions.

Once past Ax, the hills begin to close in, and past Mérens-les-Vals the climb starts, slowly at first, then hectically, as you keep an eye on the tumbling Ariège deep in the ravine below. As we rose to the height of l'Hospitalet, an awful place with a hydro-electric station, snow appeared and swathes of mist floated before us, cloaking the fearsome views of grim giants to right and left. By great 180-degree hairpin bends we struggled up to the **Col de Puymorens**, the highest so far, at 6,282 feet. We had crossed one watershed and from the top, through gaps in the mist, we could see the apparently bottomless chasm dividing us from the next, with another row of huge, soaring rock-masses to block the way. This is quite testing driving at any time of year. More convoluted twists bring you to the village of Porté-Puymorens, improbably tucked into the mountainside at an altitude of 5,331 feet, then the road straightens and begins a more sensible descent, accompanying the little stream Carol through more villages. A railway, incidentally, runs the whole length of the Ariège; it enters a tunnel under Puymorens at l'Hospitalet, emerging at Porté-Puymorens beside the Carol. We never saw a train on it.

The houses in these southern-facing villages are of grey stone, with grey slate roofs. In winter this makes them appear drab and gloomy, despite snow effects, but in late spring their walls reflect the sun and their window-boxes are gay with flowers. Some of them have curious names, such as Enveitg. The reason is that the plain beneath is the **Cerdagne**, and the people of the Cerdagne are Catalans.

The little Carol flows into the Segre, which rises in the southern watershed of the mountains beneath a height called, naturally enough, Pic de Segre, and flows north. This southern watershed is the eastern boundary between France and Spain, so for the first few miles of its course the Segre is a French river. It enters Spain about a mile south of the border-town Bourg-Madame, and has created a great high and wide basin in the mountains, called in Spanish the Cerdanya; its eastern end,

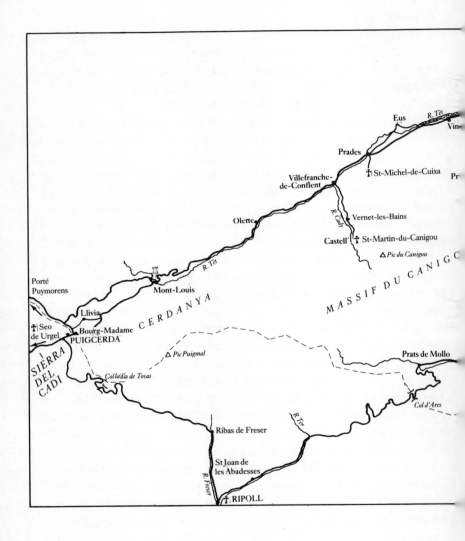

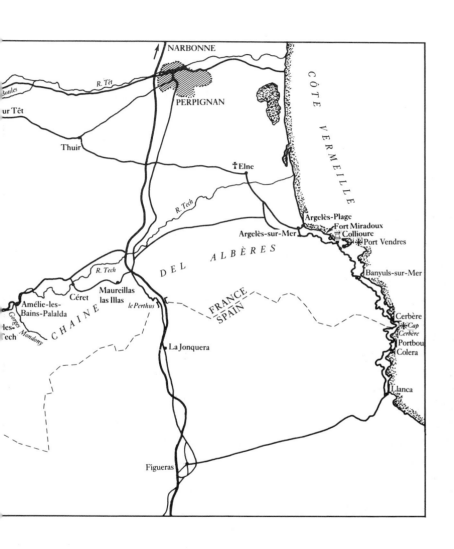

much narrower beyond the source of the Segre and terminating at Mont-Louis, is the French Cerdagne. The Segre flows west as far as Seo de Urgel, where it finds a way through the southern watershed, the Sierra del Cadi, then runs south to flow, eventually, into the Ebro, like most of these northern Spanish rivers.

The Cerdanya, the valleys of Têt and Tech, all of Roussillon, and all of the Spanish provinces of Lerida, Barcelona and Gerona, are inhabited by Catalans, who therefore occupy the entire area of the eastern Pyrenees on both sides of the frontier. They have been ruled by the French and the Spanish at various times but like the Basques are individualists who remain indifferent to national flags, preferring their own.

A short way past Enveitg, at the village of Ur (of the Pyrenees, not the Chaldees) we parted company with the railway, which went south to Bourg-Madame, and began to climb again, up to the southern flanks of the huge mass of **Carlit**, a peak of 9,583 feet; with countless subsidiary peaks, it spreads over a vast area between the northern watershed and the Cerdagne. A cluster of villages adorns this hill-road, all of them with fine views over the plain. They are all in France but also all on the edge of a little enclave of Spain around the town of Llivia, on the banks of the Segre: another Pyrenean anomaly caused by another bit of Spanish sharp-practice at the Treaty of the Pyrenees in 1659.

Still scaling the stony sides of Carlit, we arrived through the clouds at an amazingly wild, rocky wilderness called the Chaos of Targassonne, a steeply sloping, jagged mass of geological mayhem with stones strewn everywhere, as if some giant mason's stone-wagon had overturned and spilt its load. Some way beyond this, the landscape returned to civilization and we arrived in Font-Romeu.

**Font-Romeu** means 'Pilgrims' fountain'; there is such a spring here with apparently miraculous powers, to which pilgrims were wont to come, but pilgrims nowadays tend to come for the winter sports, and Font-Romeu accordingly has an astonishing collection of hotels, and like Val d'Aran, is sprouting apartment-blocks like asparagus in May. It stands in a magnificent situation at nearly 6,000 feet. A short way below the town, at a village called Odeillo, is a solar power-station, with a research-station attached. As Odeillo, Font-Romeu and the entire mountainside is south-facing, one can imagine that there is seldom a fuel shortage, and there is certainly no threat of pollution. Doubtless, however, the ski-ing season is shorter here.

North of Font-Romeu there is a place called Ermitage, with a chapel, a miraculous statue of the Virgin, and a Calvary, and it too is a shrine for pilgrimages. The fountain, in fact, is another Pyrenean mineral spring, and this and others bring invalids to Font-Romeu for treatment. By the look of the place, however, they are now heavily outnumbered by the already healthy winter-sporters.

The eastern slopes of Carlit are covered in hundreds of square miles of forest, with paths, lakes, the occasional peak, and plenty of opportunities for walks. This area is called the Capcir. J. B. Morton called it a 'strange cold upland', adding 'Summer seems but a very short interval between winter darkness and winter darkness, and the pagan gods still haunt the stony ravines and the close-set pines of Matte.' The forests attracted hunters in the past, and during the fourteenth century there was a lodge at Formiguères, the capital of the Capcir, for the kings of Majorca. This kingdom was of somewhat short duration, and began with a partition of property. Aragon was at the head of the drive to expel the Moors from Spain – King James I of Aragon cleared them out of the Balearic islands in the thirteenth century. When he died, in 1278, he split his domains between his sons, giving Aragon and Barcelona to the eldest, who became Pedro III, and Majorca, Roussillon and his feudal holding in Montpellier to the second, Jaime; this was the kingdom of Majorca. There were only three kings, who ruled it from Perpignan, the Roussillon capital, and then Aragon claimed it all back again, in 1344. The last king took his chances and went off to France to fight against the English at Crécy, and much good it did him.

We left Font-Romeu to the mist and the skiers, and motored down to the little walled town of **Mont-Louis**, known as 'the gateway to the Cerdagne'. Here the road from Font-Romeu meets one from the Capcir to the north, another from the Cerdagne to the south-west, and a fourth which departs due east and goes the full length of the valley of the River Têt. Standing at this important cross-roads, Mont-Louis was created as a military strongpoint to protect French property. The man behind the work was the celebrated engineer Vauban, and Mont-Louis shows all Vauban's skill in rendering each approach difficult, and placing a fortified barrack-block at the topmost point.

The mediaeval castle, relying on high stone walls and tall towers for its strength, had been rendered obsolete by improvements in artillery: cannon-balls could knock down such lofty targets. Alternative forms of fortification were required, and many were built. King Henry VIII of England provided a miniature example with his coastal castles of the 1540s, of which Deal, Walmer and Camber survive in the south-east, and Southsea among others along the south coast, of England. Castles now needed to be lower, with thicker walls and plenty of wide-angle fields of fire. The inefficacy of the older castles had been amply demonstrated by the English Civil Wars between 1642-1651, and the way was clear for an innovator.

Sebastian Le Prestre, Sieur de Vauban, was born in 1633 in Burgundy; he joined the army as a sapper, an engineer of mines, tunnels under enemy positions for explosive purposes. His lifetime coincided with the expansionist wars of Louis XIV, which gave him opportunities to show his skill in building rather than destroying; his talents could rise to both, because he approached the subject scientifically, using the laws of statics for building and dynamics for destroying: whatever could be destroyed should not be built, and whatever could be built, by the same laws, could not be destroyed. He rose high in the king's service, so that he became indispensable, and although he disliked war and continually requested permission from the king to retire and cultivate his land, he was denied it. He died in 1707, in the midst of the war of the Spanish Succession. It was said of Vauban that whatever he besieged, fell and whatever he built, held. When Spain joined in the first Coalition against Revolutionary France, in 1793, Spanish troops overran the Cerdagne. At Mont-Louis they were thrown back by the French garrison under one General Dagobat.

Mont-Louis has two sets of concentric walls with a deep ditch in between, and the barracks-fort at the top; within the walls the streets are laid out grid-fashion. Entrance is gained across a narrow bridge and through a dark gateway; the sloping streets of tall stone houses were quiet as we arrived because it was lunchtime. One of the town's bars supplied us with dogs, a cat, a child, two army officers, a group of locals chatting at the bar, beer and ham sandwiches. The two officers were from the garrison quartered in the fort, a training-centre for commandos. They could hardly find a tougher training ground than the forests of the Capcir and the wild and perilous slopes of Carlit. This is indeed a place to be explored with caution, supplies of food in a knapsack, plenty of surplus clothing, and a first-rate set of maps, but it can provide some wonderful walks through spectacular scenery.

We were now bound for the **Têt valley** which we approached with a certain trepidation, because Neil Lands, in *Languedoc-Roussillon*, published about a decade ago, says, the road is 'narrow, winding, and verged with a sheer drop to the valley floor far below'. Alas for romance, but hooray for motorists, the road has been widened and modernized and is no more horrendous than a motorway. Nightmare visions of a desperately narrow gorge-side track, with a heavy lorry approaching from the other direction, vanished. There is a railway here, which incredibly comes all the way up the valley from Perpignan and runs through to the Cerdagne; the skill with which it was engineered rivals Vauban's with fortifications. Below Fontpédrouse it crosses the gorge on a bridge, Pont Séjourne, which is not only brilliant functionally but aesthetically pleasing as well, with high rounded arches and slender columns. For practically the first time on any of the Pyrenean railways, we saw a train, a little two-carriage affair in red and yellow that looked like something out of a fairground. The villages in this prodigious gorge, extending for miles north-eastward from Mont-Louis, are all of the same grey stone found higher in the mountains, with slate roofs. They hang on to the gorge-side, sometimes rising quite high up the sides, diminished to the size of toys by the gigantic towering walls of the mountains on either side. Forests cling to the hillsides, too, and at the bottom, usually quite out of sight, runs the River Têt on its way to the sea.

Near the point where the gorge opens out to a much wider valley is another little walled town, **Villefranche-de-Conflent**, which gets the latter part of its name from other streams that join the Têt here. There was a town here before, unlike Mont-Louis, but Vauban re-fortified it with all his customary attention, including a little fort high on the gorge-side above it.

To testify that there was a mediaeval town here before Vauban's walls appeared, the church is twelfth-century and built of the same pink marble as the town walls and many of the houses. The romanesque doorway has delicate pink mouldings in its semi-circular tympanum; inside, the church is dark and plain except for the altars; but there are several statues, some of which are clothed, so that if you look round quickly you could mistake them for other visitors, standing and surveying the scene as quietly as you are. One of them is on its back, a supine, wooden Christ.

Some of the houses in the town's straight streets also bore witness to their mediaeval origins, and here too, like Mont-Louis, they were silent. In the little square before the church and the main gateway, the shops opened just as the church clock struck two. In the centre of this square is a pink marble platform where, on summer Sunday evenings, the populace dance the Sardane. This is a specifically Catalan dance performed by any Catalan, not just exhibition specialists, but it is not easy to learn, as Neil Lands observes: 'Many years ago, in Spain, I spent every Sunday evening for a whole summer trying to learn the Sardane. It is a step-dance, where the step changes in the middle of the bar, and the beat changes in the middle of a step. It was, and still is, quite beyond me!'

Just round the corner from the walls of the little town the railway crossed over by another bridge, the road widened and the hills receded on both sides. To the right stretched up to the clouds the flanks of the mighty **Canigou**, at 9,134 feet the last, going east, of the great Pyrenean peaks. The whole range, a great ridge on the south side of the Têt, is known as **Massif du Canigou**.

We decided to use **Prades** as our base while exploring the three monasteries of the Canigou. When we had succeeded in extricating ourselves from the vagaries of the one-way system we found an establishment called Hôtel Hostalrich. Our room, like the hotel, was bare, functional but adequate, the food simple but good.

Prades is not a particularly attractive or memorable town, although it has a church in Spanish Gothic with a late seventeenth-century retable, but for many years the famous 'cellist Pablo Casals lived here. Every year in May there is a music festival in his honour, held in the nearby abbey of **St-Michel-de-Cuixa**, one of the three monastic foundations we wanted to visit.

The abbey is a short way south of Prades. It is a working monastery, but with an interrupted history. The gentleman in the little lobby, part of the abbey buildings, spoke quite good English and directed us into the chapel opposite, built in the sixteenth century in renaissance style and now used for an exhibition of how the monastery looked originally and how the restoration work has been carried out. From this chapel you step into the cloisters, which are by themselves a very good reason for coming to St-Michel.

The first settlement on the site was made in 876, when a community of monks from St-André d'Eixalada had to leave their monastery because the Têt had overflowed and flooded it. Wisely, they chose higher ground. Nearly a hundred years later, in 974, Abbot Garin consecrated the church to St Michel, and that is substantially the church which stands now. Abbot Oliba, elected in 1009, contributed to the building of the two bell-towers (one of which still stands), the crypt and everything else in the style called romanesque. The community of monks continued here until the Revolution in 1789. The Revolutionaries were severe on monasteries because the Church as a whole was wealthy and enjoyed privileges, and the majority of French people were not wealthy and had no privileges. The monks were thrown out, their land and property confiscated, and the buildings decayed. One of the bell-towers collapsed (by 1838) and many of the columns and capitals of the twelfth-century cloister disappeared, as did the altar-stone from the church. By the time the monastery buildings were bought back and given to the Cistercians of Fontfroide, near Narbonne, in 1919, the church roof had fallen in. Restoration work had to wait until 1950, when they rebuilt the cloister and roofed in the nave of the church.

Bits of the cloister turned up all over the place, and were bought back by the monks; some pieces are still in the USA. The cloister columns, which today line nearly three sides of the square (a far greater area than that in St-Bertrand-de-Comminges) are made of the same pink marble as the whole of Villefranche-de-Conflent; polished and carved, their rosy sheen, with subtle variations, is a delight. The carvings are pagan: floral patterns, mythological beasts and geometric designs, typical of the romanesque; so is the doorway to the church, of the same pink marble as the cloister-columns and originally belonging to a tribune, an archway, from inside the church. The church itself is skilfully reconstructed: it has a long nave with aisles, and a transept which terminates at both ends in apses. Originally it had a bell-tower on each end too, but only one survives, a tall square

*The abbey of St-Michel-de-Cuixa*

tower with little windows in the style of Lombard *campaniles*. The arches are interesting because they are horseshoe-shaped, which is said to be a Visigothic characteristic. This is not so surprising as it might seem, because the Catalans are Visigothic in origin. In the presbytery the altar-stone, dedicated to St Michel in 974, has been replaced; it was located fairly recently, being used as the floor of someone's balcony in Vinca, down-river from Prades.

Relics were always of prime importance to mediaeval monasteries, because people would come to see them and pray to them, in the process usually leaving gifts to the monks. The relics at St-Michel were allegedly from Christ's crib and came in handy during the long period when pilgrims to Santiago de Compostela were travelling from all over Europe. Their southern route could involve the Têt valley and the Cerdagne, so St-Michel stood to benefit. The little buildings in the courtyard, in one of which we had bought our tickets, and the crypt originally housed the relics, but when the pilgrimages ended the relics were transferred and the crypt closed. Abbot Oliba created the crypt in the eleventh century for the pilgrim traffic, but it was filled in during the sixteenth century. It has now been unearthed and is remarkable because the entire crypt roof is supported on one pillar, in the shape of a palm tree. There is also a ventilation system, with tiny windows and shafts.

Benedictine monks are back in St-Michel now; they replaced the Cistercians in 1965. New buildings, adjacent to the old cloister, accommodate them, and I hope they can find the peace and quiet they need for contemplation; as we passed back through the chapel on our way out, a troop of Spanish schoolchildren were on their way in. And this was not the high season.

The second abbey in the region, St-Martin-du-Canigou, is accessible from Vernet-les-Bains, on the road up from Villefranche, but that would mean going back along the main road. Much to be preferred is the country lane the map showed, direct from St-Michel to Vernet-les-Bains. Direct is not perhaps the word which would occur to one after using it, since the foothills of Canigou at this point are about as direct one end to another as your average tangle of wool; it is also very narrow, so that on the rare occasions when we encountered a vehicle coming the other way, one or other of us had to manoeuvre into an infrequent passing place. One such driver, met round a sharp corner (few corners were not), was clearly incensed at meeting anyone on this road, especially foreigners. There were villages, two of them, but we met very few of their populace. The road wove a tortuous course up, down and around countless spurs and re-entrants of the hills, over a hundred rushing streams, through vast and perilous forests of greenwood trees, and once, at the top of a minor col, sprouted a steep uphill path to the left entitled 'Escala de l'Ours' which according to the map, can take mortals to the top of one of Canigou's subsidiary peaks, a mere 7,000 feet. The name seems to me to indicate that only bears should attempt it.

After this adventure in wild and weird lands that no normal

tourists ever cross, we arrived in the back streets of **Vernet-les-Bains** and stopped in a wide space at the side of a road within sight of the town's twelfth-century church, which backs on to its castle, and near a path which said it would ascend to a certain 'Cascade des Anglais'. Vernet-les-Bains, as one might guess from its name, is a thermal station whose waters are particularly potent in curing rheumatism, breathing difficulties and chest complaints. For some reason it was favoured at one time by English visitors, among whom Anthony Trollope and Rudyard Kipling were the most eminent. The town spills down the hill towards the river Cady as it rushes down its precipitous valley towards the Têt. There is a narrow strip of land in places at the valley's bottom, and fruit-trees are grown wherever possible.

As we were in the process of donning our walking-boots, an elderly gentleman came across and enquired where we were going. To St-Martin-du-Canigou, we said. 'Why not take the car?' he said, 'You can drive as far as Casteil, and walk from there.' The map did indeed show a very minor road leading to Casteil, and a short distance from there to the abbey: it does that because it cannot show a vertical climb in three dimensions. We said we preferred to walk. The way leads down into Vernet first, past a fine hotel called the 'Comte Wifred de Cerdanya', past the thermal station and up to Casteil.

It was about a mile and a half and the road was perfectly good, the old gentleman was quite right. Never mind, the scenery is splendid, with some fine villas on the wayside and wild, ragged pinnacles of rock overhanging the colourful orchards and pastures of the valley, the tumbling Cady audible at its centre.

Casteil was a charming village of ancient stone houses and a little church, all on top of one another up the hillside. By an attractive-looking bar, with red tables and chairs set out under the apple-trees outside, a sign-board pointed up a path to St-Martin-du-Canigou, 'l'Abbaye'. Round the corner was another hairpin bend and a sheer wall of rock, rising high above Casteil, and another stream crashing through a deep gorge between towering rock-faces to the right. There was no sign of the abbey, not a solitary stone of it, and the hill here was only a shoulder to carry the path on still farther.

We climbed for three-quarters of an hour, endlessly upward, and came upon a tiny chapel with a stupendous view over the valley, and another notice promising that the abbey was only another ten minutes' walk. The path zig-zagged up through the woods and then we were there, at the Abbey of St-Martin-du-Canigou. What neither of the signs had mentioned were opening hours. The abbey was closed. Another couple were sitting up there, dazed and silent, as if stunned by exhaustion, or rendered mute and immobile by some mad monk's curse.

Mist was drifting around the great bell-tower and absides of the old abbey church, and the reconstructed buildings behind it: great care had evidently gone into the restoration, begun as long ago as 1902, when a bishop of Perpignan took the trouble to start repairing the damage caused by the elements; the monks here had been driven out by Revolutionary malice, just like their neighbours at St-Michel.

In the year 1051, a messenger made a long and arduous journey from this high and remote eyrie, to all the monastic foundations he could trace or hear of – through these eastern Pyrenean valleys, along the south coast of France through all the old Roman towns, to Arles, then to Poitiers, Tours and Orleans, to Paris and northeast to Soissons and the Meuse to Maastricht. When he came to people of German speech, he went as far as Aachen, then along the Rhine to Coblenz, up the Moselle, to Metz, returning into France through the Auvergne, then travelling south and back to the Canigou.

This nameless man was bearing the news that Count Wifred of Cerdanya, the founder of this Abbey of St-Martin, had died there in 1050; and he took with him to all the abbeys and priories along his route a roll of parchment on which he asked them to attach their sentiments and prayers on hearing of Wifred's death. When the parchment was filled, the sympathetic monks, very few of whom had ever heard of Count Wifred, stitched on extra lengths of parchment recording their condolences in the flowery, grandiose prose of the age. For example, the following entry was made by the monks of the Benedictine monastery of Grasse, in the diocese of Carcassonne: 'When, on the last day of April, the fulgent orb of Titan had reached its western bourne, your messenger with wordy scroll came to us announcing the deaths of Wifred and others of your Fathers. Which when we heard, we prayed the One and Trinal God, that he would give them now a heavenly robe, and as the prophetic voices here foretold, two hereafter when the Last Day comes, that throughout endless ages they may sing hymns and praises to the Lamb.' The roll of parchment was kept, and we are fortunate to peep through this window into a different world, 900 years ago, when it was considered that prayers for the soul of a good and worthy man were worth a journey on foot of a thousand miles or more.

The county of Cerdanya was a typically post-Carolingian phenomenon. During the hundred years after Charlemagne's death, his great empire disintegrated. Counts, appointed by him or his son and grandsons to administer remote territories along the 'marches' of their ramshackle empire, made themselves little kingdoms with hereditary rights, in the Germanic fashion. And several, also in the Frankish tradition, partitioned their territory between their sons when they died. No orders came from the king, after 888 not a single legislative measure was issued from him involving public interest. No national taxes were demanded, even to buy off marauding Northmen, so there was nothing to stop Count Wifred the Hairy, one such royal representative at just this period, from acting as he thought fit. He was count, not only of Barcelona, but of other Catalan regions such as Gerona, Ausona, Urgel, Cerdanya and Besalu; on his death in 898 he distributed these among his four sons. The youngest, Miro, became count of Cerdanya and Besalu. His son, Oliba Cabreta, collecting lands from his two deceased elder brothers, gave these out among *his* four sons. The eldest, Bernard, was count of

Besalu; the second was Wifred, count of Cerdanya who founded St-Martin-du-Canigou and died there in 1050. The third was the same Oliba who was elected Abbot of St-Michel-de-Cuixa in 1009, but he had already been given the abbacy of Ripoll and the bishopric of Vich. The last son was Berenguer, bishop of Elne, who died young in 1002.

Count Wifred's monks of St-Martin wrote an eulogy to him when he died, as well as sending one of their number to advise the world of the melancholy fact. 'It is impossible to say how good he was to us while he was in the world,' they say, continuing for some while to do so in glowing terms, though adding a cautionary note: 'But since no one is made clear of sin except by god's help, especially one who has been great in the world, we pray unceasingly and with all our strength that the merciful God and just Judge will cleanse our most dear, memorable and venerated Wifred from all that he has done amiss.'

This 'good and worthy' man had done plenty amiss. Of course, it was taken for granted in his time that a nobleman should procure lucrative appointments in the Church for his sons, but Wifred went a little too far. Three of his sons might safely be given bishoprics in Urgel, Gerona and Elne – they were in his gift. Narbonne was not. At a Church Council in Toulouse, the worthy Berengar, viscount of Narbonne, had a complaint: 'My uncle was archbishop of Narbonne, and, when he died, Wifred of Cerdanya came to my parents and offered to buy the archbishopric. They held back, but my wife was Wifred's niece, and I pressed them to accept the offer. So they agreed, and Wifred gave the archbishopric to his son, who was then a boy of ten. But it is not this that I want to complain about, but about his conduct since he became archbishop . . .'

This was 1056, and trouble with the Pope was to ensue.

The bell-tower of Count Wifred's abbey stands firmly, like the rock it is made from and on which it has stood since the archbishop of Narbonne was ten years old. It has a recent embellishment, a fine wood-carving, dated 1979, of St Martin himself, cutting his cloak in half and giving part of it to a beggar. Martin was a soldier in the mid-fourth century in the Roman army, but the incident with the beggar was followed by dreams of Christ, and he left the army to follow St Hilary. Later he founded a monastery at Poitiers, became bishop of Tours, and spread the Gospel around the Gallic countryside.

The third of Canigou's monasteries is the Priory of Serrabone. We left Prades on the highway, down-valley towards Perpignan, with the snowy head of Canigou striking the sky to the right; across the river was the village of Eus, perched high on the hillside, white walls and russet roofs and a stone church tower. Near Vinca is a lake, long, tree-lined and tranquil, made by damming the river, then there is a turning to Bouleternère. The lane is typically Pyrenean. It snakes along the side of a deep gorge made by a river called Boules. According to signs, it led eventually to a village called Boules d'Amant, which may have a printable translation; or not. There are remarkably few houses along this road, although one or two ruins, and those that were still tenanted seemed to us to be as lonely and isolated as any hermit could desire. Outside one a red-haired woman was hanging out washing, while a child and two dogs romped about in the grassy paddock before the house. There were no neighbours except the large dark birds, hawks or perhaps buzzards, circling slowly above the hills and treetops.

The **Priory of Serrabone** is set high on a hilltop like St-Martin but is nevertheless a good deal more accessible, because the road to it is wide enough to drive all the way up without hazard or reversing around each corner. We were the first visitors of the day. There was a car-park, a short walk, and there was the little church, standing starkly above the deep river-gorge. Two men were working on some restoration of an inconspicuous kind; when we entered the little vaulted office-room and rang a bell it was some time before anyone came. Then a young lady emerged, she was the curator, and had only just arrived. She took our entrance fee, and we admired the tiny

*The priory of Serrabone*

cloister, just one row of beautifully carved columns and a little open walk below from which one could survey the deep, solemn quietness of the mountains, the tree-filled gorge, the rounded, foliated hillsides.

Why did they always build their monasteries at the top of hills? Because St Benedict, who wrote a rule-book for the conduct of monasteries and the behaviour of monks in them, decreed that the best place to found one would be as far away from the inhabited world as possible. If a community of monks lived on the top of a hill, miles from the nearest town and as difficult as possible to approach, they were unlikely to be disturbed. After all, their purpose was the contemplation of God, meditation on the teachings of Christ, prayer and worship, and the pursuit of a life in the imitation of Christ's precepts. To attain this they must be untouched by any of the distractions and temptations of society with others; they must see no women, have no money or any other possessions, and obey the will of God, as expressed by their abbot or prior.

Serrabone was founded for Augustinian Canons in the early eleventh century, by the same Count Wifred of Cerdanya who was responsible for St-Martin-du-Canigou. In fact, if it was intended for Augustinian Canons by Count Wifred, he must have been far more up-to-date in the latest of Church movements than seems likely in a remote and provincial ruler, because Augustinians hardly existed before mid-century when Wifred died, and only came into prominence between 1075 and about 1125. They were a breakaway group of much deeper intellectual pretensions than the Benedictines, taking the writings of the fourth-century St Augustine (*Confessions* and *City of God*, for example) as their basis, and actually studying the Bible. They eschewed the severe strictness of the Benedictines, with their unswerving discipline and endless succession of liturgical interruptions to meditation and study. Information is sparse, but if Count Wifred founded Serrabone as a priory, it was probably for a colony from St-Martin: the canons would have occupied it at a later date.

At all events, the buildings and the carvings therein are very similar to those at St-Michel: the same roseate marble, carved with stylistic animal and foliage designs, faces of humans and creatures. Inside the dark, simple church, there is a tribune, also of this wonderful marble, with such a wealth of the same romanesque carving that it could provide an education in the style on its own. The curator switched on the lights for us, and they illuminate to magical effect the glowing beauty of this work.

Within the church, and inaptly situated at its eastern end where the altar should have been, was a display of cork carvings by one Claude Massé, ugly pagan figures with huge eyes and arms outstretched. There is no shortage of cork hereabouts, for the forests are full of *chêne-liége*, the cork-oak. We paused for a while on the little ambulatory below the cloister, to appreciate the quiet beauty of this monastic refuge.

Once down from the hill, we found a country road through flat orchard land, cherry, plum and apple trees, all in blossom, and regained the main road near Ille-sur-Têt, turning right and heading for Thuir. This is the flat river plain, near the coast, but looking right you can still see the craggy white head of Canigou. It is the heart of vine-growing Roussillon, and the whole landscape is striped with rows of vines, in all their stages of growth, graced by numerous placards proclaiming that they belong to Côtes de Roussillon. Crossing over the south-bound motorway called La Catalane, and the main road to Perpignan, we drove into **Elne**, because at the top of its hill, rearing above the river-plain, is a fine cathedral well worth seeing.

A rise of 170 feet is not exciting compared with giants like Canigou and the rest of the High Pyrenees, but in a flat coastal plain it is a commanding height. Hannibal camped on this hill when taking his army out of Spain and along the south of France to Italy, but more of him later. Elne became a local capital called Illiberis and from the fourth century on was known as Castrum Helenae, in honour of the Emperor Constantine's mother.

Constantine I had clawed and fought his way to the sole possession of the imperial throne after the failure of Diocletian's Tetrarchy, the system of a college of emperors: two were to rule east and west, with the title of Augustus. Each should choose a deputy, called a Caesar, and after a period of twenty years should resign; each Caesar should be promoted to Augustus, and each of those should choose a new Caesar, and so on. The system broke down as soon as the first twenty years were up, in 305, because one of the original Augusti, Maximian, was reluctant to resign. There was civil war. Maximian's Caesar was Constantius Chlorus, who was in Britain at the time and died the following year. His soldiers acclaimed Constantius's son, Constantine, as Augustus, rather than Caesar, but it took him six years of fighting to confirm it. Immediately before his decisive victory against his last rival, Maxentius, at the Milvian Bridge at Rome, Constantine had dreamed and seen a vision of the Christian cross, hearing a voice say that the Christian God would protect him. He told his soldiers to paint on their shields the Christian symbol known variously as the Labarum or the Chi-rho symbol, consisting of the Greek letters *chi* and *rho*, the first two in Greek of Christ's name. This symbol is carved in stone in the cloister at Elne.

Constantine's mother Helena was a barmaid from Bithynia, in Asia Minor, who had become his father's wife or mistress before he was made Maximian's Caesar. She atoned for a somewhat unholy persecution of her step-children (those of Constantius's second wife, who had replaced her), not to mention a suspicion of involvement in the death of her daughter-in-law, by travelling in 326 to the Holy Land and building magnificent churches in the Holy places, Bethlehem and Jerusalem – at imperial expense. She is even said to have found the True Cross. She died, aged about 80, on her return to Rome in 330.

A bishop was early established in Elne – there may have been a bishop enthroned when one of Constantine's sons, Constans, came here in 350 – but the present cathedral dates from only 1069. Tradition has it that Constans was murdered in Elne; if so, he was on the run. As emperor of the West, he had been ineffectual and pleasure-loving, and his own commanders turned on him, one of them proclaiming himself emperor in his stead at Autun, in central France, while Constans was on a hunting expedition nearby. It is a long way from Autun to Elne, but traditions often have some substance.

The cathedral of Elne is no longer a cathedral. It stands on the crest of the hill, high, handsome and romanesque, but its bishop was moved to Perpignan in 1602. His palace has a cloister attached, with even better carvings on its capitals than St-Michel and Serrabone. Time your visit well, the place is closed between 11.30 am and 2.00 pm. And don't think you'll be able to eat, unless you bring your own picnic.

Having descended steeply from the cathedral's plateau at the top of the town to the principal street at the foot of the ramparts, where a street market was just breaking up and moving away, we looked into the least offensive of a row of somewhat insalubrious bars and asked for the usual café lunch: nothing doing. So we moved to another, and another, and yet more, walking all over town, following one set of directions or another. The best restaurants were all closed, so were the worst, and not one of the bars could offer so much as a baguette and a lump of cheese.

We took the road south, across the river Tech near its mouth, and drove into Argelès-sur-Mer. This town is not 'sur-Mer' any more, and neither is Elne, although both used to be, centuries ago: the sea has receded. From Argelès we went to dip our toes in the blue Mediterranean.

# 8

# The Côte Vermeille

Argelès-sur-Mer, Collioure and all the other towns and villages on the coast as far south as the border with Spain, are on the extreme edge of the Pyrenees. The two Pyrenean rivers which flow eastwards to the Mediterranean, the Têt and the Tech, split the range. Between the two is the Massif du Canigou, and to the south of the Tech is a range of hills called the Chaine des Albères, which terminates in the sea. Because their rock is a rusty red colour, which transfers also to the soil, the coast-line here is called Côte Vermeille, the Vermilion Coast. A road snakes its way along, connecting the towns, and at one time it carried some heavy traffic, which it shared with its fellow from Perpignan to Spain, over the low pass 'le Perthus', farther west. The motorway 'la Catalane' has taken the brunt of it from them both, so it is possible to enjoy the coast once more. The difficulty is knowing when to enjoy it, because during the summer the most attractive towns, like Collioure, become seething tourist-traps, and I shall relate what happens when you go too early.

**Argelès-Plage** really is 'sur Mer', with a long sweep of beautiful sandy beach, fringed by forests of pines and cork-oaks. For most of the year the sea is that deep violet that comes when the sun is at its height and no cloud dares to venture across its face.

Around the cliffs to the west is Collioure. The road climbs up and over the Albères, wriggles a few times, then dives down into the bay between two forts, Miradoux and St-Elme. Beyond the great, grey Templars' castle we saw a couple of hotels on the far side of Plage de la Balette. One of them, painted pink, had a bedroom with a balcony overlooking the bay, and a glass-fronted restaurant where the lucky residents could take their dinner and their ease, watching the lamps reflecting in the dark water, below the velvety black silhouette of the old castle. It was ideal.

The castle, which opens in the afternoon at 2.30, flies a flag with narrow horizontal red and yellow stripes, not the *Tricolore*: this is Roussillon, and the colours are those of Catalonia.

The Visigoths came from eastern Europe and, because of pressure from other east European tribes, such as the savage Huns, newly arrived from the Asian steppes, they took advantage of Roman military weakness in the late fourth century to help themselves to imperial land – along with Ostragoths, Vandals, Burgundians, Lombards and Franks. They established a power base at Toulouse and settled on both sides of the eastern Pyrenees in the Toulousain, Gothia and large areas of Spain. Gothia became known as Gothalunia, later as Catalonia.

There is nothing very Visigothic, however, about the language the Catalans speak. It is a dialect of the Langue d'Oc, the Latin spoken by provincials in the south of Rome's western empire. There were three kinds of Latin dialect. The Langue de Si was spoken in Italy, the Langue d'Oc in southern France and Spain, and the Langue d'Oïl in northern France. The names come simply from the way the speakers said 'yes', for which there is no word in Latin. In Italy they said *sic (si)* which literally means 'this'. In southern France they said *hoc* or 'that', and in northern France *hoc illud*, a barbaric combination, meaning basically 'that thing'. *Hoc* became *oc*, *hoc illud* elided to *oïl* and later to *oui*. French unification has meant the virtual elimination of the Langue d'Oc, despite efforts to revive Provençal, but the Catalans insist

*The Templars' castle at Collioure*

on their dialect, in Roussillon as well as Spanish Catalonia.

Collioure's castle is called Château Royal. It was massively built in stone, mainly in the Middle Ages, with an immensely high curtain wall rising from the water's edge, and a great square tower. It was built by the Knights Templar against the ravages of Saracen pirates, the scourge of the Mediterranean throughout much of the Middle Ages. The Templars were one of the two great military orders raised in Jerusalem, in 1118, when the knights of the First Crusade had established their little Latin Kingdom of Jerusalem in the Holy Land. A knight from Champagne, Hugh of Payens, was probably the originator of the idea of a fighting order on the lines of the recently established Knights of the Hospital of St John, for the purpose of keeping the road from the coast to Jerusalem free from bandits. He received permission from King Baldwin I to instal himself and his companions in a wing of the royal palace in Jerusalem's Temple area. Members of the order were expected, like monks, to take the vows of poverty, chastity and obedience, but they were also pledged to fight for the defence of the Holy Land. They were in three grades; the knights, who were of noble birth; the sergeants, from merchant families, who were grooms and stewards; and the clerics, who were non-combatant chaplains. Their badge was the red cross worn on a white tunic over armour by the knights, and on a black tunic by the sergeants. They recruited many members from western Europe, and in time the Order waxed wealthy as landowners, wishing to obtain salvation for their sins, willed land to it. The little kingdom lost its capital, Jerusalem, in 1187, and in 1291 it was ousted from the last remaining coastal stronghold. 'Outremer', as it had been called, was dead. The Templars by this time had become bankers, and their wealth, coupled with their obedience to the Pope rather than to any secular ruler, excited the passions of King Philip IV of France, *le roi de fer*, who extinguished the Order with all the systematic mendacity and hideous cruelty that we in the twentieth century can associate with Hitler and Stalin.

Château Royal was re-fortified as a frontier bastion by Vauban, whose work can be detected in the area behind it, in the late seventeenth century, and if you go to Collioure in, say, May, before the crowds multiply too thickly, you may be able to enter it and see it all by yourself.

The Hostellerie des Templiers nearby has an extensive and cavernous saloon bar, its walls smothered in paintings, drawings, etchings, sketches, of all sizes and degrees of quality, by a myriad of unknown artists. At the next table to us, a once-varnished, plain wooden piece like all the chairs, several elderly gentlemen were playing cards and shouting at each other in the quacking, harsh, nasal tones of the Catalan tongue. The bar itself was shaped like the side of a boat, the only concession to trendy modern tourist-attraction in the place.

The Hostellerie has a tradition to maintain. Not only the bar walls are papered by paintings, so is the staircase, right up to the top floor, and so is the restaurant. The reason for this patronage of art is that, in 1905, some painters congregated in Collioure, created a new kind of painting style, and left some of their work to be hung in the Hostellerie.

Rouault and Matisse had already met when studying with Gustave Moreau, in 1892. Matisse brought Derain with him to Collioure in 1905, and there they met Rouault and Vlaminck, a friend of Derain. Together, in the vivid light and inviting images of this little fishing-port, they experimented with form and colour, carrying their conception to the ultimate in economy and expression. They exhibited in the Salon d'Automne in 1906 and created a sensation from which the group gained the name 'Fauves', because one critic likened them and their work to wild beasts.

'Fauvism came about,' said Matisse, 'because we excluded all imitative colours, and because we obtained more powerful reactions with pure colours – stronger simultaneous reactions; and it was concerned furthermore with the luminosity of colours.' Like Gauguin's work, Fauvism involved an arbitrary way of using pure colours in flat areas, invoking imagination rather than reality. Matisse called the kind of harmony thus created 'spiritual space'. One of the best examples of the technique, painted by Matisse in Collioure, is his 'Still Life with a Red Carpet' in the Musée des Beaux-Arts in Grenoble. These revolutions in painting techniques, repulsive as they may be to people who like pictures to look like something they recognize, are necessary when a tradition of painting becomes ossified into a series of stale imitations. A fresh start, however horrifying to those who prefer what they know, breaks new ground and permits again spontaneity, with the valuable acquisition of additional technical knowledge.

The paintings here were in fact in many styles, from Fauvist to Impressionistic to realistic. They included Collioure scenes and landscapes, seascapes, portraits, nudes, and a wide selection of attempted cubist and surrealist studies. Some were good, according to our inexpert judgement, some mediocre, some frightful, but they provided immense interest, as no doubt they

*The church and* phare *at Collioure*

have done since the Fauvists offered some of theirs to the Hostellerie's *patron* in payment for a meal or drinks or lodging.

The church, a seventeenth-century building dedicated to St-Vincent, has incorporated the ancient stone *phare* or lighthouse at the harbour-mouth as its campanile and clock-tower. The principal feature of the interior, which is otherwise very dark and plain, is the massive retable or altar-piece, occupying the entire west end from floor to ceiling, in three stages of flamboyant Baroque. This is the majestic masterpiece of the Catalan sculptor Joseph Soñer of Manreza, who constructed similar altars in many Roussillon churches. He started work in 1698 and it took him three years. Lights have to be fed with francs to illuminate it. There are eight side-chapels, all with similarly grandiose altars to various saints.

Along the foreshore fishing-boats were drawn up and commandos were performing exercises in beaching and launching their rubber boats. A waterside bar on Plage de la Balette bears on its walls some old photographs of the bay when the fishing-boats used to be drawn up on the

154

beach by the dozen, with huge lateen sails furled.

That evening, the bay looked just as it should, with the lights reflected in the water, and the castle and lighthouse silhouetted. The hotel's restaurant was full of people, the atmosphere was convivial, the prospect picturesque, the meal delicious. We went along to Café le Petit Faubourg for a nightcap, and the patron entertained us with good-humoured badinage, with other customers and ourselves. He was patently a character, and when we left refused to let us pay for our wine. On the subject of wine, there is a wine co-operative's *cave* in a former Dominican friary near the hotel, from which I bought some Collioure red and some 'Vieux Banyuls', a heavy, slightly sweet wine, excellent as an aperitif.

Collioure is known as 'the pearl of the Côte Vermeille', because it is easily the most attractive of the ports along this shore. The latter might well have been called 'Côte Romaine' instead, because so many of the towns have Roman origins. Collioure was Cauco Illiberis, Port-Vendres was Portus Veneris, and Cerbère was Cerberus. The majority existed before the Romans occupied them for, as Belloc reminds us, 'Rome made of the barbarians a new world, but before she began that task Rome had inherited everywhere within a march of the Mediterranean a belt of land whose civilization was similar to, always as old as, and sometimes older than, her own.'

**Port-Vendres** is a ferry-port for the North African trade, with a number of quite big ships at its quaysides and a vast terminus building. It too is a holiday resort, however, as is practically anywhere on this highly picturesque, mountainous coast. The road wriggles and turns right and left like a frenetic earwig before gaining the crest of another extrusion of the hills into the sea, and arriving at another bay and another seaside town, **Banyuls**. The Catalan sculptor, Aristide Maillol, lived here so we stopped and searched for the town hall, as I knew that behind it stood his war memorial. Many towns in Roussillon, like Perpignan and Céret, have examples of Maillol's work, which often consists of a nude of generous proportions and formidable thighs; he used his wife as a model, which accounts for such consistency.

Banyuls' sea-promenade boasts an old cannon, an aquarium, a laboratory for the study of marine biology, and facilities for yachting and bathing and seaside holidaying. The town also has a Wine Festival in August each year.

The coast road, with its wicked corners and steep gradients and the blue, choppy, Mediterranean on its left (most of the time), continues to behave as if it were a permanent guest at a wine festival all the way to **Cerbère**. This small, pleasant resort, whose eponymous mythical character was the three-headed dog Cerberus guarding the entrance to Hades, is the last town before the Spanish border. The road, however, has to perform another intestinal convolution out to Cap Cerbère and back inland again, climbing all the while, until it reaches Puerto d'Els Balitres and Spain, descending the last outcrop of the eastern Pyrenees, the southern, vineyard-terraced hillsides of the Albères; here the soil and rock take on a pale orange shade. We skirted the little towns Portbou and Colera (which could be difficult to advertize as a holiday resort) and left the road at Llanca, heading back towards the sea and a last look at the Mediterranean, before going back to the mountains.

# 9

# *Le Perthus, Céret and the Ripolles*

Before we left the little bay, the fig-tree beneath which we had been sitting, the prickly pear, the umbrella pines, the whole delicious Mediterranean ambience, we went to the Restaurant Farella. A modern, light, ground-floor room with windows all around, it was already filling up and the waitresses were hard-put to keep us all served. There was a long tableful of workmen, eight or nine of them, and some were not bothering with a 'beaker full of the warm south', they were squirting the blood-red nectar straight into their mouths from a gourd.

The gourd is made of goat's skin with the hair inside. Its top is made of goat's horn, about half an inch across, and the nozzle, also of goat's horn, screws on to it with a tiny hole through which one drinks. There is also a stopper for the nozzle. To fill the gourd you remove the nozzle and pour the wine in through a funnel. To drink without using a receptacle, you remove the stopper, take the top horn-piece in your left hand and hold the gourd, squeezing slightly, with your right. The thin stream of wine should be directed from the tiny hole straight into your mouth, but you must not swallow, you have to pour the wine straight down your throat. Then you relax the pressure of your right hand, tilt the gourd upright at the same time and stick your left forefinger over the tiny hole. All this takes some learning and the beginner will make an appalling mess the first few hundred times he tries. But the benefits are enormous, they say, for you do not need a glass and furthermore, as Belloc says, 'it is designed by Heaven to prevent any man abusing God's great gift of wine; for the goat's hair inside gives to wine so appalling a taste that a man will only take of it exactly what is necessary for his needs'.

We now headed inland, for Figueras, leaving the Albères on our right for a dead-straight road across a plain, which seemed truly representative of Spain: wide open spaces, plenty of sky, a good deal of aridity about the landscape. There was also much irrigation about it, too, and crops were growing in all the fields. Figueras looked like a big, modern, busy town, so we threaded our way through it to find the road to France and the pass over the Albères called le Perthus.

The road we took was the old one, N11, becoming N9 in France: the new motorway kept it company at a short distance all the way, taking off the bulk of the heavy traffic. As it left the plain, entering the low foothills of the Albères, the scenery became rougher, the hills covered in scrub and small scraggy trees, and there was no sign of cultivation anywhere. On hilltops appeared gigantic black bulls in wooden cut-outs, to show the traveller from France that he was now in the land of the *tauromaquia*. We passed by the village of La Jonquera, set apart from the roadside cafés for the truck-drivers, as if it was trying not to be seen with them. The cafés were a mild foretaste of the excruciating vulgarity of the cluster of shops, *bureaux-de-change*, bars, amusement arcades, and other paradisic delights at the crest of the low pass of **le Perthus**. At only 951 feet, this is a piece of cake compared with all the other Pyrenean passes, even for the elephants in Hannibal's army, which did not have to contend with customs sheds, policemen and all the enticements of today's funfair.

During the third century BC, two powers were locked in conflict in the Mediterranean: a familiar attrition which has characterized international relations through the ages. Should Carthage enjoy the monopoly of Mediterranean trade, or should

Rome? Carthage was the older power, with trading-ports from one end of the inland sea to the other, but Rome was energetic, up and coming, and determined to overcome all opposition to its rise to pre-eminence. In 218 BC, war came again, and Hannibal Barca, Carthage's most capable commander, was in Spain; the Romans had endangered Carthaginian influence there and Hannibal had responded by attacking and capturing Saguntum, held by a tribe allied to Rome. Hannibal was consequently expecting a Roman army to be despatched to Spain, and he crossed the Ebro from New Carthage (Cartagena) to meet them in Catalonia. With a force of over 100,000 men and 40 elephants, he subdued the northern tribes between the Ebro and the Pyrenees by the end of June, and waited for the Romans. But they did not come. There had been a rebellion of the Celts in northern Italy against Roman colonies there, and the legions intended for Scipio's expedition to Spain had to be diverted to deal with it. By September it was clear that the Romans were not going to come, so Hannibal reduced his force to 50,000 infantry, about 9,000 cavalry and 37 elephants, and prepared to march swiftly into Italy to strike suddenly, unexpectedly, at Rome's colonies and bring their subject tribes over to his side against them.

This was the force that crossed the Pyrenees at le Perthus; the first camp on the far side was at Illiberis (Elne).

A coalition of Gallic tribes was prepared to contest his passage through their territory at an *oppidum* called Ruscino, east of modern Perpignan on the south bank of the Têt; known today as Château Roussillon, it gave the province its name. Hannibal won over the chieftains, however, persuading them to co-operate with him, and continued his rapid march across southern Gaul. How he crossed the Alps into Italy, and what happened to him, his army and his elephants in the long campaign that followed, need not concern us. Rome won the struggle and, in the hundred years that followed Hannibal's gallant attempt to stop them, consolidated their hold on southern Gaul and Spain. In the late second century BC, the governor of Provence, the oldest Roman province outside Italy, was Domitius Ahenobarbus, and it was he who established a new province to its west, Gallia Narbonensis, and built a road to connect it with both Spain and Rome. This road, known as the Via Domitia, ran from the western end of Provence at Tarascon, through Nemausus (Nîmes), Narbo Martius (Narbonne) and Elne, and is the same road that crosses the Pyrenees at le Perthus.

Quite soon, cutting through the Albères down to the Tech valley, a turning to the left leads to a village called Maureillas-las-Illas, and Céret. The valley here, quite wide between the Albères and the Massif du Canigou, was a beautiful sea of pink and white orchard-blossom. Soon we were in **Céret**, with an immediate problem of where to park, for even in April cars were everywhere and vacant parking places nowhere. Eventually, remembering Pau, we parked almost on a pedestrian crossing, and found the superb Hôtel des Pyrénées in a side street not far away.

The first objective of any visit to Céret must be the **art gallery** in the Rue Joseph Parayre to the left of the Hôtel de Ville. Céret, like Collioure, saw the birth of a new art movement.

Pablo Picasso was born in Malaga on the Mediterranean coast of Spain in 1881. His father, José Ruiz Blasco, was a painter of modest talent but young Pablo showed far more. As a young man, using his mother's maiden name, Picasso, he moved to Paris and lived among other painters and poets with his mistress, in a building called the 'Bâteau-Lavoir' in Montmartre. He knew Matisse, Derain and Vlaminck but when, in 1907, he painted 'Les Demoiselles d'Avignon' (now in New York), everyone was horrified except another friend, Braque. Picasso had been to Collioure with the 'Fauves', but in 1908 he moved with Braque to Céret, into the mountains, to try further developments of style and technique. 'I do not paint what I see,' said Picasso, 'I paint what I know.' He and Braque, 'roped together like mountaineers', as Braque put it, explored the possibilities of abstraction, but found by 1911 that their new style was becoming too abstract and too hermetic in its perfection. They introduced both real objects to the surface of their paintings, and colour, which had almost vanished. This was the inception of Cubism, which has led to a dozen other experiments in artistic techniques in the years since then.

The ground floor of the Musée des Arts Modernes is devoted to truly modern artists (dated 1986), the first floor to their distinguished predecessors. There is a room full of Picasso sketches and drawings, some of which are inscribed by him 'Drawn for the Musée in Céret'; and a glass case with ceramic bowls by him, in orange, yellow, and black, showing vivid and dramatic scenes from the bullring. There are some typically lunatic Dalis, some eccentric Jóan Miros, some pleasant Chagall lithographs, a sketch by Picasso of Manuel Hugue Manolo and a portrait by him of Etienne Terrus, a bust of whom in stone we had seen on the cathedral terrace in Elne, because he was a painter from that town.

It is worth spending some time exploring the streets of the old town, hidden behind the walls but accessible through aged gateways. The church is originally twelfth-century but full of Baroque mouldings and paintings and a big retable, all somewhat delapidated and seedy. Narrow alleys between the tall, old, stone houses, lead to a quiet square with a 'Fountain of the Nine Jets', and eventually to Place Pablo Picasso, where you can sit in the sun outside Bar Pablo.

Bits of Céret's fortifications remain here and there to demonstrate its erstwhile strategic importance: the Tech valley narrows beyond this point, so it guarded the upper valley, known as Haut Vallespir. There is a mediaeval bridge, restored in the eighteenth century, called Pont du Diable (the satanic personage seems to have been responsible for a great many bridges, gorges, and mountains in the Pyrenees, probably out of spite for his failure to tempt the Basques).

Leaving Céret, head up-valley between the heightening mountain-sides to **Amélie-les-Bains-Palalda**, a cumbersome name easily explained: Amélie-les-Bains is on one side of the Tech, Palalda on the other. Both have thermal stations and both were Roman foundations. Palalda was Palatinum Dani, and parts of the original Roman building are still visible in Amélie's 'Thermes Romaines'. Amélie used to be called Arles-les-Bains until 1840, when it was renamed in honour of Queen Amélie, consort of King Louis-Philippe. The whole place was nearly wiped off the map just a hundred years later. In October 1940, 30 inches of rain fell in three days, the floodwaters rose over 30 feet and swept down the Tech valley, carrying everything away. Roads vanished, the upper valley was cut off, and Amélie-les-Bains nearly drowned. Even the dams thrown up by the débris washed down by the heavy rain broke, and another mountainous wave tore through the valley. Amélie-les-Bains caught the worst of it, which is why most of its buildings are fairly new. Its capacity for curing rheumatism and asthma is unabated, however, and it has some good walking nearby, notably to the Gorges Mondony to its south. A Vaubanesque fort guards the approach to the town from down-valley.

A mile or two farther on lies **Arles-sur-Tech**, which evidently escaped the worst of the 1940 flooding because its houses are very old, set so close together that you can hardly get a bicycle, let alone a car, between them. We stopped there, and followed one of the chasmal streets to a gateway giving access to the Abbey Church of Ste-Marie, which has a cloister intact. As it dates from the eleventh century, the column capitals have the same kind of romanesque animal-carving as St-Michel-de-Cuixa and Serra-bone. The church, like most romanesque churches, is dark, with tiny, high, round-headed windows, and one of the altars looks as if it might be the work of Joseph Soñer. The little abbey church used to be the religious centre for the Vallespir, and is one of the oldest in Roussillon.

Just outside Arles a path leads off to the right, into the cliff-like hills on the southern flanks of Canigou, to the Gorges de la Fou. They can only be visited on foot, as an excursion for someone staying at Arles, or Amélie, and despite their name one does not have to be mad to go there. The cliffs on either side of the gorge are multi-coloured, like those of the Tarn, and the river that created them falls into the Tech, no doubt a fearsome sight during those floods of 1940.

Above Arles, the valley narrows still more, the orchards give way to pasture, then to a rugged wilderness; beyond a village called le Tech there is a deep gorge called the 'Défile de la Baillanouse', and then there is the last town of the valley, **Prats-de-Mollo**, clinging to the hillside on the edge of the tumultuous river. In fact the river is fed by several sources and one of them separates the upper from the lower town, connected by an old pack-horse bridge called Pont Guilhem. The whole place is fortified, and cars cannot enter through the gateways or pass the narrow streets, so it is a haven of relative peace. One of the mediaeval houses is called 'Maison des Rois d'Aragon', because those monarchs built it, when they wanted some holiday refuge, in the days before the Treaty of the Pyrenees determined that Prats-de-Mollo must be in France. As a frontier town it was further fortified by the ubiquitous Vauban, and his fort stands above it on the steep hillside, Fort Lagarde. From the far side of the river you may enjoy the view of the town walls, the fort above them and the imperturbable head of Canigou in the distance, raised over all.

The climb out of the Tech valley begins immediately one leaves Prats-de-Mollo, giving superb views of the lovely Vallespir, down what seemed to be its full length, and almost of the sea. On a clear day, it must be possible. All around, once more, were the snowy mountaintops, across the valley, and old Canigou. Up among the rocks, we crossed a couple of minor cols then climbed again, above the snow-line, to Col d'Ares, at 4,963 feet, where the bored frontier-men waved us through, and we were in Spain again.

The view down the valley of the Ter was beautiful; there was no traffic on the road, and we could see nothing moving. The serenity of the mountains was upon us again. The first town on the Spanish side was Mollo. A short way farther on lies Camprodon, which has the shell of a monastery church and in its parish church a statue of a Virgin, which is the object of a local cult. **Sant Joan de les Abadesses** has another monastery. Count Wifred the Hairy of Cerdanya founded it, in the ninth century, for nuns, and the first of the *abadesses* was his daughter, Doña Emma. When the present church was built, in the twelfth century, the Augustinian canons took it over, and the best of the carvings – a fourteenth-century tomb of the Blessed Miro and a thirteenth-century group depicting, in wood, the Descent from the Cross – are from their time. In the town we saw the ruin of a romanesque church, but that was certainly not the monastery; there was nothing to indicate how we could go to it, and my Spanish was not up to asking. The town was small but bright, and apparently derives its living from making all the sausage-skins in Spain.

The valley of the Ter is green, cultivated, wide and pleasant. Together with the valley of the Freser, it comprises a district known as the Ripolles, because the two rivers meet at the town of Ripoll; the Ter is the first river of the Spanish Pyrenees, going eastward, that empties itself in the Mediterranean sea instead of joining the Ebro. The Ripolles is the heartland of Catalonia, in the province of Gerona, the city which lies up-river of the Ter's junction with the sea, and it embodies the traditional Catalan genius for combining primitive peasant agriculture with energetic enterprise in trade and commerce, particularly in iron-working, as we shall see.

We drove into **Ripoll** and found ourselves exactly where we wanted to be, in the square before the imposing Ayuntamiento, the town hall, the church and monastery, and the tall stone building housing the museum. A little old man sold us a ticket to park in the square, and as it was lunch-time we set off in search of some suitable source of sustenance. We found it after crossing the wide, turbulent Ter and an ancient rusty single-track railway: 'La Trobada', a truly excellent bar-restaurant-hotel.

Neither church nor museum opens until 3 pm. Eventually a little bearded man arrived at 3.10 and unlocked the **museum**, so we went to that first. It is housed on the top floor of the ancient stone structure at right-angles to the church and displays aspects of local Ripollese life, with their religious emblems, models wearing ladies' dresses in the finest of lace, and a row of heads sporting variations of the mountain Catalans' red cloth caps. The pride of Ripoll, however, was the iron industry, and there was a full-scale model of an iron forge, with men working in it. Many of the artefacts produced by the local forges were on display – farm tools, horseshoes, carpenters' tools, locks and keys, and a large number of muskets and pistols, the manufacture of which developed into a large local industry. All labels and notices in the museum were in Catalan and Spanish, and one of them, as far as we could gather, proclaimed that from the sixteenth to the eighteenth centuries, Ripoll was one of the most important arms-producing centres in Europe. Iron-forges were widespread in the Catalan Pyrenees, as one may tell from the frequency of 'Farga', which means forge, as a place-name: an obvious example is La Farga de Moles, on the border of Andorra, but there are numerous others, less conspicuous.

The museum was spacious and absorbing but on the whole it could have been set out more attractively and its notices could have been couched at least in one other language, perhaps French, for the benefit of those who are not conversant with either Spanish or Catalan. One exception, however, must be made to this stricture. As we left, the curator showed us a small wooden object vaguely like a whistle, and a card which, in Catalan and no less than three eccentric translations, explained that it was a portable, pocket sundial:

> We should specially call your attention concerning this portable sundial called 'the shepherd's'. It is a cylinder, as long as it is necessary, and with the corresponding diameter, with a hoop on top to be hung from. From top

to botton it has twenty lines which divide the perimeter in twelve equal segments, one for every month of the year, and a series of helicoidal curves playing the role of an horary: downeards for the hours in the morning, upwards for those in the afternoon. At the topside there is a rotating piece provided with a protunding rod, used as a gnomon. In roder to know the time the top slinding piece must be rotated until the gnomon coincides with the date; afterwards, the whole cylinder is orientated towards the Sun until the shadow falls vertically: the end of the shadow indicates the time.

Huge glass doors had been installed to protect, from a distance of perhaps fifteen feet, the lovely romanesque twelfth-century porch of the **Abbey Church of Santa Maria**, and the space between new doors and old is roofed. Having entered the patio-space, there is a fee to see the cloisters which, like the tympanum over the porch, are a masterpiece. They are complete in their square, and what distinguishes them is that the original twelfth-century columns and capitals, in violet jasper, had superimposed on them in the fifteenth century an upper gallery of columns in granite, so that there is a double arcade of double columns, 440 of them in all.

The first monastery on this site was founded by one Reccared, the first king of the Visigoths to become a Catholic. The Visigoths were Arians until the sixth century, having been converted in their earlier homelands in eastern Europe by one Ulfila in the fourth century. Ulfila, consecrated bishop in 341, invented a Gothic alphabet for the Visigoths and translated the Bible in it, but he was an Arian, so the Visigoths were converted to this heresy instead of orthodox Christianity. The early controversies in the eastern Church had centred round the argument of one Arius, a presbyter of Alexandria, that Christ, having been made man, must be metaphysically and morally inferior to the Father, and belonged to the created order. Orthodox bishops protested that this idea undermined the whole

*The cloisters at Ripoll*

point of Christ's sacrifice to save human souls, since if He was not wholly divine then He had no authority to do so. The controversy split the eastern Church for many years, and Arianism took a serious hold, with the unfortunate result that missionaries like Ulfila spread an ignorant and heretical version of the faith among barbarian tribes like the Visigoths. The Goths, who originally stemmed from Gottland in southern Sweden, moved across Europe when the Roman Empire in the west was unable to stop them. The Ostrogoths invaded and conquered Italy itself, the Visigoths ventured farther west and established their kingdom of southern France and most of Spain.

Reccared's Catholic monastery of the sixth century was destroyed after a fairly short existence, during the fighting between Moor and Christian in the eighth century. It remained for the redoubtable Count Wifred the Hairy to refound it, for Benedictine monks, in 888. It was his great-grandson Oliba, however (brother of the Count Wifred who founded St-Martin-du-Canigou, abbot of St-Michel-de-Cuixa, and made abbot of Ripoll in 1008), who established its reputation for academic eminence.

Santa Maria was a family monastery, their responsibility, their pride and also their mausoleum; so Oliba, princely prelate (he was bishop of Vich, the next town down-river from Ripoll as well), patronized his houses generously. He corresponded with the scholars of the great abbey of Fleury on the Loire, he visited Rome and returned with papal permission to embellish the monastic services, and although he does not appear to have been much of a scholar himself, he encouraged others to reside in his abbey of Ripoll, so that in time it became a reputed centre of learning, with writers producing works on music, arithmetic and chronology. Its library, remarkably extensive for the eleventh century, remained almost intact until a terrible fire in 1835 destroyed it. Some volumes from Oliba's time survived, but many irreplaceable works vanished. Because of the fire, much of the fabric of the inside of the church at Ripoll had to be restored, but it is still impressive, if not outstandingly easy on the eye: it is vast but very plain, with walls of stone ashlar, reminding us of some immense station on the London Underground. It has the chill of all ancient stone buildings, contrasting with the afternoon warmth outside.

The road followed the River Freser upstream, accompanied by a railway, complete for once with a blue and yellow train. The mountains closed in on either side. **Ribas de Freser**, set about the steep banks of the torrential river, is a truly Pyrenean town. 'Is there anywhere in the world,' asks J. B. Morton, 'where you can know more fully the meaning of rest than at Ribas, where the torrent rushes beneath the window of the hotel?' Well, yes, actually; I have tried to sleep in places where a torrent rushes beneath the window, and it isn't easy. Today winter-sports have taken a hold in Ribas, but higher up in the mountains, in the *Reserva Nacional de Freser i Setcases*, under the shadow of the mighty Puigmal, is Nuria. Since the eleventh century, the time of Count Wifred and his brother Oliba, there has been a sanctuary of the Blessed Virgin there, and although the church is not older than the seventeenth century, it is still the second most popular

Virgin in Catalonia. The mountain railway from Ribas will take you there.

Puigmal, at 9,547 feet, is higher than Canigou, and it is part of the watershed which here is the frontier with France. At Ribas de Freser the road turns ninety degrees and climbs sharply to cross it, into the Spanish Cerdanya.

# 10

# *The Cerdanya*

It is a long, slow ascent to the snow-line, with Puigmal looming up on the right. The Pyrenean range here, hemming in from the south the plain of Cerdanya, is called Sierra del Cadi, a name recalling the long struggle against the alien forces of Islam. The Pass of Tosas, 'Collada de Toses' in Catalan, is at 5,905 feet and at the col stands a large and very new hotel, for the skiers. The descent, like the climb the other side, has fewer break-neck hairpin bends than usual, just long, easy downhill stretches, into the flat, open country of the Cerdanya, full of pasture, horses and fruit trees. As the road crosses the Segre and enters a long straight run slightly uphill, the town of Puigcerda is visible at its end. Skirting Puigcerda, we made for the stretch of neutral highway between it and Bourg-Madame on the French side of the frontier, and on to the Spanish town of **Llivia**.

When the French and Spanish politicians were wrangling about the frontier in 1659, the Spaniards yet again managed to slip the French a fast one, in the same way as they had wangled continued control over Val d'Aran. The French had won control of Roussillon, and Cardinal Mazarin wanted to be sure of access to it over the Pass of Puymorens, down Val Carol and by way of Mont-Louis down the Têt to Perpignan. Included in this should be all the villages along the way. Certainly, said the Spanish diplomats: the head-waters of the Segre, the upper Cerdanya and all its villages should henceforth be French. Llivia, however, was not a village: it had a charter and could prove that it had always been a town. Was it not, after all, the old Julia Livia which, as capital of the Cerdanya in the days of the great Roman Empire, had been granted municipal status? The French could not deny it, so Llivia, with a little hinterland around it, stayed Spanish, and this bit of road, with customs posts at the Puigcerda end, was made to go from Spain, into France, and into Spain again.

Llivia has many new apartment-blocks of the Val d'Aran type springing up within its territory, presumably for the benefit of holiday-makers and not for the Llivians. Judging by the houses of the old town, the native population is still most likely to be around 1,000. Their houses are mainly of stone, lining narrow streets leading up to the church at the top; some of them have a Swiss look, with deep eaves and balconies. The church clock chimed 10.15 am as we walked back down the steep little lanes between ancient dwellings and store-houses. It was Sunday, and few people were about, but that did not prevent the grocery store from opening. We shopped there for wine and a bottle of Ricard, amazed at how little we had to spend for it. With prices like those, no wonder French people come here for holidays, and no wonder new apartments and hotels are being built for them.

**Puigcerda** does not present a remarkably attractive face to the world, since although of mediaeval beginnings, it has had more than its fair share of destruction by fire. It was founded in 1177, when King Alfonso II of Aragon, having received the Cerdanya from his father the count of Barcelona, decided to build a summer residence there. Its situation, as a town, is extremely vulnerable, so it has been attacked and sacked in virtually every century up to the twentieth, when the Civil War of 1936-39 once more laid it waste. Had it been a French frontier town, then Vauban would have fortified it.

Spurning the unfortunate town, therefore, we took the road along the northern side of the Cerdanya: the only road that connects Puigcerda with Seo de Urgel, and in doing so were in for a surprise.

The Cerdanya is an upland plain, created by the attempt of the Segre to find a way out and prevented by the intervention of the Sierra del Cadi, running parallel with the Pyrenean watershed. It is high (Puigcerda stands at 3,780 feet) but fertile, and famous for its horses, the greatest breeds in Spain. The Ceretana mare, sired by the French Percheron, bred powerful cart-horses; sired by a Breton stallion, she produced the best gun-horses in Europe. Crossed with the donkeys of Vich, she gave mules that transported the merchant goods of all Spain.

We saw plenty of these big Cerdanya horses as we motored along the pleasant Segre-side road among vivid green pastures. Deep gorges channelled river and road from Isobol to Bellver, then the plain broadened again; we were enjoying the splendour of Sierra del Cadi to our left, and the rapidly rising banks to the unseen Pyrenean heights to our right, when at Martinet came the aforesaid surprise, prepared for us by the Spanish road authorities.

In most countries, the said authorities being solemn, pragmatic and businesslike, when they are rebuilding a road, they leave a section of the carriage-way in reasonable order and channel the traffic through it. If the traffic is heavy, it takes time, because only one-way is possible: some entertain the motorists with pretty coloured traffic-lights which change to a deep, admirable red just when they think they are getting somewhere. The motorists, nevertheless, although exceedingly bored, arrive at the other end with only the consumption of petrol altered.

The Spanish are not satisfied with this dull treatment: they want the drivers to have all the fun of the fair, so they convert the road into an adventure playground. Having constructed new sections of the road, with freshly bored tunnels in the gorge-rock, away from the old road, all ready to be used, they were determined, on this C1313, to give us all a jolly time before letting us use them. So they had started to rip up the surface, leaving about half a mile at a time with just a gravelly, stony, dusty rubble-heap to drive along. They punctuated these stretches with a length of the original tarmac, simply taking care to rip that into shreds by moving heavy plant along it, so that deep trenches, holes and ridges, cracks and crevasses appeared at every yard. It was only about twelve miles, after all, and through some superb scenery, so why not slow down to ten miles an hour? Even if the drivers themselves have to concentrate very hard in their endeavour to avoid the worst of the chasms and stones, swerving violently and peering myopically through the swirling dust spurted up by the car in front, what unparalleled pleasure for the passengers, not only to see the beauties of the gorges, if they can make them out through the yellow clouds of dust, but to have an exciting ride at the same time! Happier still those who tow caravans, with an excellent chance to replace all that dreary crockery, which they would soon have to do; and what thrills for the motor-cyclists and opportunities to display their skills, just like a scramble. The pillion-passengers might never experience anything like it again. They might not survive it.

When it is finished, the C1313 will be a road of unsurpassable brilliance, and traffic will be able to flash along from Bellver to Seo de Urgel without noticing the natural beauty. But the authorities are making them wait a long, long time.

It was only half a mile before the outskirts of **Seo de Urgel** that the road resumed its normal, boring nature, and we accelerated to a nervous 25 mph, fearing instant disintegration if we exceeded it. In Seo we parked in a street off the centre of things, and made for the nearest bar. On the wall was a coat-of-arms in painted wood. We could not discover why it was, that while the Catalonian flag consisted of horizontal stripes of red and yellow, in the coat-of-arms the stripes were vertical; a badge in this form appeared on the rear of many Catalonian cars. Beneath this specimen was enscrolled the word 'GATALUNYA'.

It was Palm Sunday, and some of the families entering the bar included little girls and boys all in white, bearing palms in highly elaborate designs, mainly made from plastic, by the look of them. When we left this exceedingly hospitable haven and made our way, by streets off the highway, to the older part of the town and the cathedral, we saw many more families in similar dress, especially in a little terraced playground before the cathedral.

The buildings in Calle Mayor were stately and elegant, tall, stone-built and pierced on the ground floor by deep arcades which in the hot summer afford soothing sanctuary from the sun. The **cathedral** stands at the edge of the town, with fine views down the Segre, for it is at Seo de Urgel that the river turns south, finding a way around the flanks of the Sierra del Cadi, making for the Ebro. Mass was about to begin at the cathedral, so we did not enter but gazed instead at the fine twelfth-century romanesque porch and the apse, surmounted by a gallery of arches in the same characteristic style.

Seo means cathedral: the see of Urgel, the seat of a bishop. From the days of the Visigothic kingdom there had been a town, a cathedral and a bishop, until the seventh century. Then came the tidal flood of Islam, advancing through Spain from North Africa, engulfing the Pyrenees and washing into France to be checked at Poitiers in 732 by Charles Martel, the 'Hammer'. For 50 years the Mohammedans held Septimania, the southern kingdom including Roussillon and Catalonia, with Narbonne as its capital, but political stability was as elusive to the Moslems as it was to the Christians in the Middle Ages. In 839 the cathedral in Urgel was consecrated when the Moors were evicted, and from that time forward the bishops were in the forefront of the Reconquista. Not, it must be added hastily, that there was much urgency in this project. The Moors brought higher standards of civilization, literacy and tolerance to Spain than the Christians had known since the days of the Roman world. In Moslem Spain, Moors, Jews and Christians were encouraged to live together without persecution by one sect of another. Scholars studied subjects such as mathematics and astronomy that were denied to the Church-ridden Christians; works of the Greek masters,

Aristotle, Plato, Euclid, Pythagoras, had been translated by the Arabs and Christian scholars came to Toledo and Cordoba to translate them from Arabic into Latin, to make them accessible to Europeans.

It was only when the Caliphate of Cordoba collapsed with the death of Almanzor in 1002 that the idea of a 'crusade' to drive the Moors from Spain became current, and it was not until mid-century that the possibilities of conquering the Moslem *taifas*, the local governors who had continued after central government from Cordoba had faded, were put into practice by King Ferdinand I of Léon-Castile. Then came the crusading enthusiasm of the Franks, backed by the Pope, the same Alexander II who gave Duke William of Normandy his blessing for the invasion and conquest of England. The Frankish knights, as barbaric and ignorant as they were when they invaded Roman Gaul 600 years before, saw it as a campaign against the wicked Moslems, merely cattle for slaughter. It was this myopic zeal which gave birth to 'The Song of Roland', and it was an embarrassment to the Spaniards, who were coping with the Moors adequately enough without such fanaticism. Both Alfonso VI of Léon-Castile and his great warrior-general, Rodrigo Diaz, 'El Cid', were capable of making alliances with sections of the Moors when it suited them.

In 1085 Alfonso captured Toledo, but the Moors revived with a fresh invasion from North Africa. When the Cid died in 1099 and Alfonso ten years later, leadership of the Reconquista passed to Aragon and Barcelona. When Queen Petronilla of Aragon married Count Raymond-Berengar of Barcelona, who was also lord of Provence, and her son Alfonso II joined all these territories together to form one kingdom, there was a substantial and unified Christian power in the north-east of Spain. The commercial wealth and energy of Catalonia ensured that Aragon should be strong, and together with the kingdoms of Castile and Portugal, all ruled by Alfonsos, the Moors were guaranteed a long and troubled period before them. There were no fanatical crusades but a more or less constant effort, sometimes involving other kingdoms like Navarre, which took no further part after the victory of Las Navas de Tolosa in 1212. Eventually Islam was evicted from its last stronghold, Granada, far to the south.

The cathedral of Urgel has cloisters and a diocesan **museum**, the door to which is at right angles to the porch. It is even open on Sundays from 10 am to 1 pm and has a remarkable collection of mediaeval documents, including the Act of Consecration of the cathedral in 839. The prize exhibit is a manuscript of about AD 1000 which is a commentary on the 'Apocalypse' of the Blessed One of Liebana, in 93 folios. The principal attraction is in the illustrations, which look something like the products of Hieronymus Bosch's bleak imagination. Another manuscript, of 938 'in the second year of Abderrahman, King of Cordoba', is an exposition of the Dialogues of St Gregory. There is also a papal Bull of Pope Sylvester II, the great scholar Gerbert of Auvergne, who aided and abetted the Emperor Otto III in his abortive attempt to recreate the Roman Empire, around the same period of 'l'an mil', about which there were sundry misgivings in contemporary Europe, and predictions of Armageddon. This particular edict from Sylvester defines and confirms all the rights and possessions of the dioceses of Urgel, 'ita ut nullus Rex, nullus Princeps, nullus Comes, nullus Marchio, nullus judex, nulla magna parvaque persona', should infringe them. Powers and principalities beware: the bishop of Urgel, his rights and lands and properties are untouchable.

One of these latter is the reason why Andorra is still independent, and the nature of the edict helps to explain why the bishops of Urgel are and have been so important in Pyrenean politics. One of the most prominent was St Ermengol: fortified by the Papal Bull, he defended and extended his see, and began the building of the present cathedral, but it was not finished until 1175. The cloisters, three sides of which survive, are of the same date.

Urgel (in Catalan, La Seu d'Urgell) is a more elegant,

spacious, sedate and satisfying town than Ripoll, and you could spend much time in it, admiring the beauties of the old houses, and the streets with their stately and cool arcades; but now we are heading for Andorra, and the last part of our travels.

# 11

# *Andorra*

As a boy, I used to see the tiny triangle of Andorra on the map and wonder at so small a place being an independent state, like Monaco and Liechtenstein. The idea of it caught my imagination, and I found out all I could (which was not much) from such meagre references as *Whitaker's Almanac*. I even attempted an essay about it, but could not extend it beyond a page of a school exercise-book. A mountain principality, overlooked by modern nation-states, a remote valley in the Pyrenees where time has stood still, surely this would be the most romantic of all places for a traveller to visit.

The independence of Andorra was an accident, born of mediaeval feudal confusion. As it developed from shadowy origins in the tenth century, when western Europe came under attack from all quarters, the feudal system, as it has been called, filled up with chaotic uncertainties and absurd anomalies. Charlemagne's Frankish Empire had disintegrated into a thousand petty states where each appointed rural officer, like the counts of Foix and Cerdanya, the Viscounts of Béarn, seized the chance to consolidate his own authority and pass on his property to his eldest son, or even divide it among his several sons. Then, in the ninth and tenth centuries, came ferocious assaults on a primitive society by marauding Moors or Saracens from the south, by the terrible Norsemen from the northern seas, and by tribes such as the Magyars from the Asian east. Poor country-folk looked to their lord for protection, the count, viscount or duke who had assumed authority over them. He gave them protection, as far as he could, with his armed followers but in return demanded their land, for which they had to pay with some kind of service. The system of vassalage, each man being another man's vassal, his faithful follower, redistributed what had been a more or less lateral society (land shared out in family groups) into a vertical one, with infinite degrees of vassalage. A man could hold his land from a local minor lord, a man-at-arms, who was vassal of a viscount, who held his land from a count, who was vassal to a duke, who was the king's faithful liegeman. In between, at all stages, came the Church, which held land for its needs and could be a kind of corporate vassal to any duke, count or king. The greatest difference between a lay lord and the Church was this: that a man might die without issue, or leaving only daughters who would carry the land to another lord, their husband; the Church never died, so that if land came under the control of an abbey or a bishop, it stayed there for ever.

The valleys of Andorra, remote, poor, and unimportant, were subject to feudal lords like every other valley and town in the Pyrenees. There was a count of Urgel and one of Castellbo, a valley with a village of no great size to its west (turn off C1313 a couple of miles south-west of Seo de Urgel, to your right). The counts of Castellbo for a while were powerful, allied to lords on both sides of the Pyrenees, and frequently a nuisance to the bishops of Urgel. At some time in the eleventh century, when Wifred was count of Cerdanya, and his brother Oliba the pluralist abbot of both Ripoll and St-Michel-de-Cuixa and bishop of Vich, a count of Castellbo either inherited or was granted authoritative rights over the Valleys of Andorra; unfortunately for a coherent explanation but luckily for the Andorrans, as it turned out, these rights had been held by the count of Urgel and he never renounced them; nor did the bishops of Urgel, when the counts bequeathed them to the Church.

In due course the counts of Castellbo vanished from the scene, and Andorra might well have remained simply a minor and undistinguished possession of the bishops of Urgel. Many other valleys, such as Castellbo, followed that pattern, to be absorbed into one or another of the great nation-states of France and Spain which emerged in the sixteenth century. However, Arnaud, the last count of Castellbo, having no son, married his only daughter Ermendessa to Count Roger-Bernard of Foix (an ancestor of the Roger-Bernard III who inherited Béarn along with *his* wife). With Ermendessa went the rights over Andorra.

A kind of contract, or statement of rights (called 'Pariatge' in Catalan), was signed by the bishops of Urgel and the count of Foix in 1278. It converted Andorra into a *Dominion Indivis* shared equally between the two lords as co-princes: the Valleys now comprised a principality. When the count of Foix-Béarn, also king of Navarre, became King Henri IV of France in 1589, his rights passed to the Crown, and the Treaty of the Pyrenees of 1659 confirmed that Andorra should forever be held by the two princes, that is, the bishop and the king. 'Forever' had no meaning for such as Robespierre, Chauvin and the other Revolutionaries, who renounced their princely rights. But, said the Andorrans, we shall be taken over by Spain and lose our individuality. Accordingly they petitioned the Emperor Napoleon in 1806, and he graciously consented to the restoration of France's sovereign rights. After the fluctuations of French politics in the nineteenth century and the establishment once again of a republic, the rights were vested in the President, with whom they remain. The Spanish prince is still the bishop of Urgel; the Church never dies.

During most of this time Andorra was governed by an elected Council-General, granted to them by the co-sovereigns in 1419, which makes Andorra's one of the oldest parliaments in Europe. It did not make it the most up-to-date: not until 1933 did all Andorran males over 25 get the right to vote, and only in 1970 did women vote for the first time. The meeting-house for the Council-General is 'La Casa de la Vall' in Andorra la Vella, as it has been for 400 years.

To reach the capital take the road from Seo de Urgel that accompanies the River Valira upstream. At the frontier village of La Farga de Moles, beyond the customs sheds, are two large supermarkets of recent construction, both open for business even on a Sunday. Cafés, bars, shops and petrol stations line the road and merge with the first village, Sant Julia de Loria, also enslaved to the gods of commerce. We drove along a very narrow gorge, through which the Valira thrusts out of the upland plain in proper Pyrenean fashion: Sant Julia was the first town of Andorra. Santa Coloma came and went, and then we were in **Andorra la Vella**, looking as usual for somewhere to park and a suitable hotel, of which there is no shortage. In the main street, Avenida Santa Coloma, we settled on Hotel Bell-Pi and parked outside, half on the pavement, half in the road. There are no proper car parks, it seems.

There is not much of the 'old' part of town left. On every side new buildings loomed, geared to the making of money. For centuries Andorra lived from its meagure agricultural products, its people hard, proud, stoutly independent and tough as nails. The valleys are all way above sea-level, from Andorra la Vella at 3,600 feet to La Massana at over 4,000 and Canillo over 5,000; even on fine summer evenings the atmosphere is chilly. The strips of cultivable land along the banks of the torrential streams are sometimes no more than twenty yards wide, and the produce has never been more than barely adequate to keep body and soul together. Small wonder, then, that when two profitable possibilities presented themselves, in the shape of off-duty goods and the winter-sports business, the Andorrans cashed in.

The streets are full of shops selling cameras, radios, liquor, all kinds of electrical goods and others which, being duty-free thanks to dual sovereignty, are much cheaper than in either France or Spain. Visiting a gigantic supermarket called Pyrenees, we noticed that while some of the goods were absurdly cheap, others were priced comparably with those in England, and some were much more expensive. We found the old church of Andorra la Vella, clearly much restored but showing traces of its twelfth-century origins, and a handsome promenade near it from which one may survey the whole of the valley of the Valira: it looks like the whole of Andorra, and as far as we could see there were building-sites. The valley, as a Pyrenean landscape, was irretrievably wrecked.

There was not a street in the town free from cars, parked and mobile, not only belonging to Spanish shoppers, French skiers, or visitors like ourselves, but to Andorrans too. The rain was now descending with that dour, malignant obstinacy normally associated with Test Matches at Old Trafford, and we were incensed to find that our car had been ornamented by a lady traffic-warden. It seemed we were parked on the wrong side of the road and we owed 'Comú d'Andorra la Vella' the sum of 1,000 pesetas for our *infraccion*. Several other vehicles on our side of the street had been similarly adorned and the lady was in the process of scribbling another ticket, rendered pulp almost as soon as written, for another unfortunate farther down. I moved the car down the street and parked it on the side where there was a P sign, in the last available space, removed the ticket and hoped for the best.

Bad weather and the commercial ruin of a fair mountain landscape do not give a fair impression of Andorra; the picture should never be uniformly sombre: Rembrandt preferred chiaroscura. The Andorrans are Catalans and speak Catalan, and are proud of their past. Their dual sovereignty entitles them to a choice of two kinds of postage stamp (there are French and Spanish post-boxes, side by side) and two choices of school for their children, neither of which calls for fees. They are proud, too, of their churches, several of which are twelfth-century romanesque.

There are three main valleys, created by the three principal

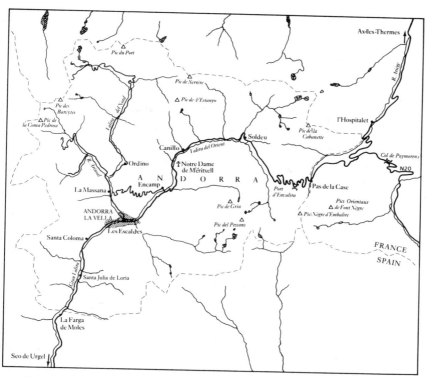

rivers which combine to make the Gran Valira: the biggest is
Valira del Orient, rising near the Envalira Pass, the only way into
France; into it at Andorra la Vella come Valira del Nord and its
tributary, Arinsal. The distance from Andorra la Vella to the Pass
of Envalira is eighteen-and-a-half miles, and from the capital to
the border with Spain about six-and-a-half. Not all of the 25
miles is spoilt by commercialism. The valleys are surrounded on
all sides by monstrous mountain peaks, all over 9,000 feet high.
To the north there are the Pics du Port, de Serrère and de
l'Estanyo; to the east, on either side of the pass, Port d'Envalira,
are Pic de la Cabanette on its northern side, Negre d'Embalire
and Pics Orientaux de Font Nègre on its southern, along with Pic
dels Pessons not far away; westward, at the head of Arinsal, there
are the giant Pics des Bareytes and la Coma Pedrosa.

There are seven parishes, though through most of its history
Andorra has only boasted six. Canillo, the highest, on the Valira

del Orient, is also the largest and oldest, and used to be the most prosperous. By right of precedence, its eldest councillor is still given the privilege of being president of the Council-General. Soldeu, the last village before the grim climb up to Envalira, is within this parish; it has been entirely taken over by the ski business: there are 23 miles of ski-slopes and twenty hotels. Not far from Canillo, and also within the parish, is the patron sanctuary of the Andorrans, the much-restored but originally twelfth-century Notre-Dame de Meritxell.

The next parish down-stream on the Valira del Orient is Encamp, in the centre of the principality and overlooked by the tall transmitting masts of Radio Andorra and the two great peaks of Griu and Pessons, cradling between them many small mountain tarns which have been put to use in a hydro-electricity plant. There is a chapel in Encamp called Santa Roma de les Bons, reconstructed in its original romanesque form.

The old Andorra can still be found in the parish of Ordino, north of Andorra la Vella, in the valley of Valira del Nord. This was the home of the old Andorran noble families, like that of Guillem d'Arény, Baron of Senaller, who introduced to the Council-General a reform act in 1866 by which its mediaeval character was brought up to date. In Ordino there is still some cultivation of the modest store of arable land and some cattle-breeding, and there is still to be found a lingering remnant of the old Andorran mountain life, the freshness of the hillside pastures, the sparkling, tumbling torrent, birdsong in the trees, flowers of all colours every spring: the other Andorra. 'No traveller,' say the Andorrans, 'will be able to say he knows Andorra if he has never visited this parish.' Quite likely, but he had better be quick. La Massana, at the confluence of Arinsal with Valira del Nord, is all winter sports, although they say that there are still some chamois in the high hills and woods.

Santa Julia de Loria is the first parish from the Spanish border, and is given up to commerce. Les Escaldes used to be part of Andorra la Vella but is now a parish on its own, called

Escaldes-Engordany; it was admitted in 1978, when the councillors in the Council-General had to be increased. Four councillors represent each parish, and for centuries there were 24: now there are 28. The thermal waters that gave Escaldes its name still exist, but the ski business is bigger: there are 50 hotels. Its chapel of Santa Roma dels Vilars is the oldest of all in the principality, claiming an eighth-ninth-century origin, but its Visigothic frescoes have been taken out and lodged in the Council Hall. Up on the hill near the Radio Andorra station is another twelfth-century chapel called San Miquel d'Engolasters.

The parish of the capital, Andorra la Vella, epitomises the difference between old and new Andorra. In 1950 there were 2,866 inhabitants, mostly engaged in agriculture and cattle-raising, with their attendant industries. Now there are upwards of 16,000, and agriculture has completely disappeared. This is where the picture loses its light and deepens into darkness, at least for those who lament the loss of landscape and old values. There are 70 hotels, over 700 shops and seven camping-sites, and it sounds like a Biblical plague of Egypt. For the Andorrans, it's eternal Christmas, for the money rolls in constantly from the off-duty shops, the hotels, the apartment blocks and the five ski-stations which rejoice in usable snow from December to May.

Envalira, or Embalire in Spanish, is the highest of all the Pyrenean passes at nearly 8,000 feet, and there is no other way of getting out of Andorra into France. For most of the long way to Envalira the road climbed, fairly gently, and progress was tedious, since it was a two-way affair with heavy traffic and local buses cultivated the habit of arriving from a side-turning just in front of us. We passed through Encamp, no longer J. B. Morton's 'corner of Arcady'. Still, at Canillo and Soldeu the landscape was less obviously commercialized than around the capital, and off the road and up the hillsides the whole sordid business could be put into perspective. Viewing man's ant-like activities from a great height, surrounded by the quiet presence of nature's works, tends to restore one's sense of balance.

Soldeu stands at 6,000 feet. Before summer, the road up there is difficult. If it rains down in the valleys, it snows up here. The snow-ploughs ram it hard down on the surface, making it slippery; snow drifts on the steep hillsides and gets whipped off by the wind, making visibility awkward. Most of the drivers, including me, dropped into second gear and crawled up at a cautious pace. The Andorrans, as if to prove that they knew the pass like the back of their skis, raced past, screeching and slithering around the hairpin corners, endangering themselves, their passengers and everybody else.

It was a long, grinding, difficult and dangerous ascent, but at last we topped the crest of Envalira. The sun had been shining hotly all the while, gleaming on the soaring heights of Cabanette, Pedrous, Carlit, Font Nègre and the rest. It is best to take the descent as circumspectly as the climb, for the violent twists of the road are hazardous. At Pas de la Case you cross into France, back to the Ariège again, past sombre l'Hospitalet, down at last below the snow, accompanying the hurrying Ariège once more to Ax-les-Thermes, Tarascon, Foix and the way back to England.

# A SHORT GLOSSARY OF
# BASQUE WORDS

Spelling is variable throughout all seven of the Basque provinces; a plural is obtained by adding the suffix k.

| | |
|---|---|
| Egunon | Good day |
| Aratzalde-on | Good afternoon |
| Gabon | Good night |
| Zer-diozu? | How are you? |
| Ongi etorriak | Welcome! (plural) |
| Plazer baduzu | Please |
| Eskarikasio | Thank you |
| Ez | Yes |
| Bai | No |
| Ona | Good |
| Gaizki | Bad |
| Ardua | Wine |
| Ogia | Bread |
| Uria | Water |
| Baita | The home of |
| Berri | New |
| Etche | House |
| Goria | Red |
| Haitza | Oak |
| Hiria | Town |
| Itsasoa | Sea |
| Mendi | Mountain |
| Ostatua | Inn |

# SELECT BIBLIOGRAPHY

Belloc, Hilaire *The Pyrenees*. (Methuen, 1909)

Borrow, George *The Bible in Spain*. (Nelson, 1843)

Brooke, Christopher *Europe in the Central Middle Ages, 962–1154*. (Longman, 1964)

Caesar, Julius *The Conquest of Gaul*. (Penguin Classics, 1951)

Caven, Brian *The Punic Wars*. (Book Club Associates edition, 1980)

Cronin, Vincent *Napoleon*. (Collins, 1971)

Dumas, Alexandre *The Three Musketeers, 8 Vols*. (1844)

Epton, Nina *Navarre*. (1957)

Froissart, Jean *Chronicles*. (Penguin Classics, 1968)

Glover, Michael *Wellington's Peninsular Victories*. (Batsford, 1963)

Halphen, Louis [in] *Cambridge Mediaeval History, Vol. III*.

Hemingway, Ernest *The Sun Also Rises* (alias *Fiesta*). (Cape, 1927)

Higham, Roger *Road to the Pyrenees*. (Dent, 1971)

Lands, Neil *Languedoc-Roussillon*. (Spurbooks, 1976)

Lavisse, E. *Histoire de France, Vol. II*.

Lehmann, Joseph *Remember you are an Englishman*. (Cape, 1977)

Morton, J. B. *The Pyrenean*. (Longman, Green, 1938)

Myhill, Henry *The Spanish Pyrenees*. (Faber & Faber, 1966)

Southern, R. W. *The Making of the Middle Ages*. (Hutchinson, 1953)

Southern, R. W. *Western Society and the Church in the Middle Ages*. (Pelican, 1970)

Tucoo-Chala, P. *Histoire de Béarn*. (Presses Univ. de France, 1962)

Anon. *The Song of Roland*. (Penguin Classics, 1957)

# INDEX

# Index

191

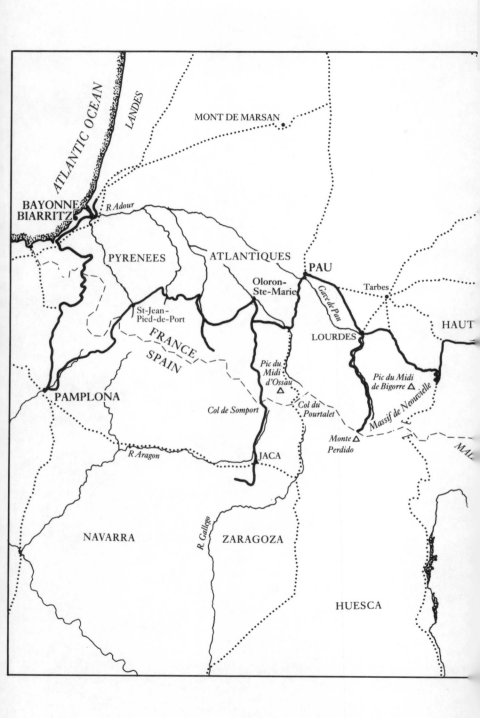

ATLANTIC OCEAN

LANDES

MONT DE MARSAN

BAYONNE
BIARRITZ

R. Adour

PYRENEES

ATLANTIQUES

PAU

Oloron-
Ste-Marie

Tarbes

St-Jean-
Pied-de-Port

FRANCE

SPAIN

LOURDES

HAUT

Gave de Pau

Pic du
Midi
d'Ossau

Pic du Midi
de Bigorre

Massif de Neouvielle

PAMPLONA

Col de Somport

Col du
Pourtalet

R. Aragon

JACA

Monte
Perdido

MAL

NAVARRA

R. Gallego

ZARAGOZA

HUESCA